Spiritual Community

Spiritual Community

THE POWER TO RESTORE HOPE, COMMITMENT AND JOY

RABBI DAVID A. TEUTSCH, PhD

For People of All Faiths, All Backgrounds

JEWISH LIGHTS Publishing

Woodstock, Vermont

SPIRITUAL COMMUNITY:

The Power to Restore Hope, Commitment and Joy

2005 First Printing
© 2005 by David A. Teutsch

Library of Congress Cataloging-in-Publication Data
Teutsch, David A., 1950–
Spiritual community: the power to restore hope, commitment and joy / by David A. Teutsch.
p. cm.
Includes bibliographical references.
ISBN 1-58023-270-1
1. Fellowship—Religious aspects—Judaism. 2. Community—Religious aspects—Judaism. 3. Jewish way of life. I. Title.
BM720.F4T48 2005
296.6—dc22
2005012156
10   9   8   7   6   5   4   3   2   1
Manufactured in the United States of America
Jacket Design: Sara Dismukes

For People of All Faiths, All Backgrounds
Published by Jewish Lights Publishing
A Division of LongHill Partners, Inc.
Sunset Farm Offices, Route 4, P.O. Box 237
Woodstock, VT 05091
Tel: (802) 457-4000   Fax: (802) 457-4004
www.jewishlights.com

Contents

Acknowledgments   vii

Preface: Recognizing Community   ix

1 Bringing People Together   1

2 A Commitment to Caring   13

3 Building Community   25

4 Radiant Centers   39

5 Becoming a Community Leader   49

6 Dealing with Conflict   59

7 Community and Spirituality   69

8 A Shared Jewish Future   81

Appendix I
Strategies for Organizing Caring Communities   93

Appendix II
Interfaith Dialogue, Religious Values,
and Public Policy   101

Suggestions for Further Reading   105

Bibliography   109

Acknowledgments

My thanks first go to Betsy, Zach, and Nomi, who supported my effort to complete this book and helped me create the space in time to work on it, and to my friends, who have indulged countless hours of conversation exploring the meaning and process of community.

The staff at Jewish Lights, ably led by publisher Stuart M. Matlins, did a wonderful job of editing and producing the book. Thanks go in particular to Emily Wichland, Mark Ogilbee, and Alys Yablon for their diligent editorial work.

My assistants Diane Schwartz and Cheryl Plumly cheerfully and ably did much of the technical work involved in producing a clean manuscript.

My thinking about community grows directly out of the Jewish communities in which I have lived. I am grateful for the nurturing I received in my first Jewish community in Salt Lake City; for the opportunity to experiment and grow afforded me by Ramat Shalom in Chestnut Ridge, New York; and for the intellectual challenges of the Upper West Side of New York City. My current Philadelphia communities—the Reconstructionist Rabbinical College and Dorshei Derekh at the Germantown Jewish Centre—have been sources of joy and challenge, learning and immeasurable support over the last eighteen years. My gratitude extends to all with whom I have shared the responsibilities and satisfactions of community.

Preface

RECOGNIZING COMMUNITY

I magine someone standing up at a congregational meeting and asking, "Well, are we a community, or aren't we?" The question implies a challenge. If we understand ourselves to be a community, then certain values, policies, and responsibilities should flow from that.

A congregant says, "If we're a community, then we need to help Susan get to the hospital for her cancer treatment." Somebody else responds, "You're right. I'll help get that organized." Somebody might say, "If we're a community, we need to have social events, and not just pray and do good works." Or, "Then we have to find Sam a new job." And somebody might respond, "Well, we're a community, but we're not *that* much of a community. We don't have the ability to get Sam a new job."

Having a community implies having both commitment and ability. There are many different kinds of commitments and abilities, and each of them varies in strength. The strength of community and the shape of community will vary depending on a large number of these variables. Many variables are beyond our individual control, but others—

especially those related to commitments, values, and ideals—
are very much in our own hands.

When I was the President of the Reconstructionist
Rabbinical College, I also served as a member of the rabbinical admissions committee. Over the years, I have had
many conversations with applicants about why they want to
study for the rabbinate. Many of them are successful lawyers,
social workers, teachers, or academicians. They say much the
same thing in different ways. They are seeking something
that is missing from their lives. They want a stronger sense of
belonging, service, tradition, and spiritual connection, and
they want to make the world a better place. Their high-pay-
ing, high-status jobs have not satisfied these less measurable
ambitions. They are now seeking the benefits that come
from building community.

I now direct the RRC Ethics Center. Recently, someone came to see me to talk about a problem. As is often the
case, I didn't know until the conversation began what it
might be about. After exchanging a few pleasantries, he said,
"I'll tell you why I'm here. I can't figure something out.
Why, if I'm so successful, am I in so much pain?" Many of us
live with a strong sense of isolation or frustration: Life just
isn't giving us the satisfaction that is supposed to come with
living the American dream. More than anything else, that is
the force driving people toward community and spirituality.
In the last few generations, most Americans have had
unprecedented freedom, mobility, education, and wealth. As
anyone familiar with the statistics on violence, drug use, and
depression knows, that has been a mixed blessing. Our
actions have been shaped by the belief that having more or
better possessions and greater financial security will make us

happier. That was the key to our thinking during most of the modern period. In our current postmodern, postindustrial age, many people are questioning that assumption and hoping to forge better lives. I think that by creating community—a strong, vibrant community of shared living and shared passions—we can achieve that lofty goal.

Underlying the drive for community are several disparate yet complementary desires. Some people are looking for close friends; others hope to find a permanent companion to love and share life with. Some come to community to overcome loneliness; others come for a shared cultural, social, or spiritual life; still others are seeking support. Some come knowing they have much to give.

But community transforms everyone, often in unexpected ways. Teachers become students; students turn into teachers. Those poised to give of themselves often find they derive more from community membership than they give.

In community we find strength in what we give, receive, and share. And in a strong community, we share a great deal—life rhythms, values, and a way of living. That kind of sharing infuses life with meaning and richness not found any other way.

Through community my kids have become friendly with dozens of adults who live lives worth emulating. They are surrounded by people concerned about their welfare, people who celebrate their development and correct their misbehavior. Community also means dinner invitations, shared festival celebrations, friendships, and roots.

I sought out community for shared Jewish living. Only the passage of more than thirty years has shown me how much greater and how much more diverse than I ever imagined are the gifts that community living bestows.

THE ORIGIN OF SHARED LIVING

Human nature was forged in clan and tribal settings. If people had not naturally adapted to the values and practices of the tribe, the human race would not have survived, because internal dissension would have kept the tribe (the critical economic and defense unit) from functioning effectively. Imagine, for example, what would happen to a hunting party if its members didn't cooperate.

Hardwired into human consciousness is acceptance of the authority of clan leaders and a willingness to internalize the leader's vision; that allows the clan to function effectively. As a result of this deep human patterning, we only feel good when our way of living harmonizes with the lives of those with whom we maintain regular social contact—our peer group. When we do not share our daily lives with people who support our values, we feel embattled and undermined. When there is dissonance, we unconsciously seek to eliminate it. We need to share our lives with people who reinforce our values and beliefs.

If we want to teach ideals and beliefs, values, rights, and responsibilities, then we need clan-size groups to do the job.

Early clans were small social groups with mutual interests, strong interpersonal connections, and a common history, culture, values, and economic life. Today, strong communities resemble these early clans in many regards— they are a primary grouping of people who are tightly connected and who share values, goals, and responsibility for one another. In this book, I focus on how we can create vibrant local congregations that share many of the characteristics of these strong communities.

THE SHATTERING OF CONNECTION

When clans were the primary form of human organization, they functioned as communities in the strong sense. When small villages became the primary form of social organization, interpersonal connection and commitment were almost as powerful, and these communities were truly successful. But as cities grew in size, smaller social structures usually developed within them to meet the needs that the larger entity could not fulfill. Synagogues and churches, guilds and markets, schools and military units are all examples of such mediating structures. They all imbue small groups of people with a sense of community, compensating for the city's mass culture and anonymity, which eroded community life.

Over the last few centuries, industrialization has brought rapid social change. For efficiency, cities became increasingly large, and smaller economic units broke up. The high rate of mobility shattered many people's links to the groups with which they had a shared history and culture. Extended families that had run farms, trading companies, and other enterprises ceased functioning as the primary economic unit.

New modes of communication and transportation meant that individuals had regular contact with many more people. The emphasis on material values and consumerism combined with such passive entertainments as movies, television, radio, and recorded music to increase our isolation. The stability, duration, and intimacy of the earlier kind of community were no longer accessible to most citizens of industrial society.

Support for individual autonomy figured prominently in this shift in social structure, giving ideological support to the economic changes required by industrialization. Autonomy and individual choice—the hallmarks of modern society—have brought us unprecedented personal freedom, yet they have struck a blow to community building. No longer do we feel obligated to honor the community's right to demand loyalty and to assert that we must sustain community, even when that involves personal hardship.

Most residents of contemporary American society live with that loss. It is expressed in feelings of depression or isolation, and in uncontrolled aggression and antisocial actions like vandalism, cheating, and petty theft. Why don't we express our loss more clearly and then do something about it? I'd like to suggest three reasons: First of all, most of us have never experienced community in the strong sense, so we don't know what we're missing. Second, the term *community* is so frequently used in a restricted sense (e.g., medical community, Irish community, Los Angeles community, virtual community) that most of us have become cynical about it. Third, the maintenance of community appears to conflict with our privacy, personal freedom, and economic opportunity, and perhaps to require significant effort.

And so, unfortunately, many of us live most of our lives outside clan and community, lives limited by shallow roots in tradition and heritage.

RESTORING CONNECTION

It's hard to imagine that we will ever return to living in clan structures, and almost as hard to imagine living in preindustrial villages. That is particularly so in the United States, where autonomy and the rights of the individual have become the basis for our self-identity.

If we are to live in real communities again, they will have to be intentionally created substructures within the larger political and economic structures of postindustrial society. Since communities are a primary source for our lifestyles, friendships, and moral values, creating such communities will require us to figure out how we want to live, what we believe in, what we want our lives to be about.

When we apply this thinking to the goal of creating new Jewish communities, it is important to note the language that many communal leaders use to define their groups. As a synagogue consultant for the last thirty-five years, I have come to understand the power of the metaphors invoked by this language.

For example, board members sometimes talk about the congregation as a family and sometimes as a business. The *family* metaphor spotlights the need for friendship, intimacy, and mutual responsibility. The *business* metaphor focuses on efficiency, effectiveness, and attention to financial issues.

While both these metaphors reflect elements of congregational life, they are too narrow. Unlike a family, members of a congregation do not automatically have a bond to each other or accept any mutual responsibility for one another's well-being. Unlike a business, a congregation does not have financial profit as a primary concern. The missing idea, it seems to me, is that of the congregation as a community. The community must be concerned with the well-being and interconnection of its members, as it must be with its economic stability. This idea of congregation as community encompasses all these functions without the distorting aspects of the other metaphors. But because the term *community* is so frequently used in its more limited sense, the challenge before us is to help our leaders recapture the full meaning and promise of strong community—and to reimagine the possibility that our local congregations can themselves become strong, vibrant communities based on shared rituals, values, relationships, and mutual responsibility.

BRINGING PEOPLE TOGETHER

FINDING OUR WAY HOME

Remember the old saying, "Home is the place where, when you get there, they gotta take you in?" An astonishingly large number of people I meet don't have that kind of home. As somebody on a TV talk show put it, "If he came home in that condition, I'd toss him out on his ear." But we all want to come home—home to a place of safety, to a place where, when you get there, they gotta take you in.

A real community is that kind of home. It understands that, as it says in Genesis, we are all created in the image of God, that every human being is a creature of infinite worth, even though it doesn't seem that way sometimes. Maintaining membership in a real community doesn't hinge on exams or measurable output. It does depend on accepting responsibility for citizenship within the community. Before we can define the role of a citizen, we need to examine what a community is and what it does.

When communities are functioning well, they take care of their own members. It is important to distinguish between the feeling of community, what Jonathan Woocher calls *communitas,* and an actual, existing community. You can have a moment of *communitas* in many different situations— a *Kol Nidre* service, a baby naming, singing "The Star-Spangled Banner" before a championship ball game, or singing "Auld Lang Syne" on New Year's Eve.

The feeling of *communitas,* of human closeness and belonging, is a wonderful thing. It can happen any time people share a powerful moment, good or bad. But by its very nature, it is transitory. In that way *communitas* is unlike community, which involves a commitment to sustaining relationships of trust and caring over time. Community is a source of *communitas,* but is also stable and durable. No sense settling for just a feeling of belonging when you can have the real thing.

THE FUNCTIONS OF A COMMUNITY

In many institutions, such as corporations and factories, caring doesn't extend too far beyond the institution's walls and prescribed hours. But a full community is not subject to those kinds of limits. Most institutions fall between what the prominent liturgy scholar Lawrence Hoffman has called *minimum-liability* and *maximum-liability* institutions.

In a minimum-liability institution, people join for very specific benefits but have no obligations beyond those required to gain the sought-after benefits. Country clubs, Boy Scout troops, and many congregations are examples of minimum-liability institutions. They provide specific functions—golf, meals, weekly meetings and trips, religious services, counseling, and so on. Outside their area of agreed-upon responsibility, they need have no concern. While it may make for more pleasant golf games if everyone at the club shares similar backgrounds and views, ample evidence exists that liberals and conservatives, Democrats and Republicans, businesspeople and academics can happily coexist in the same country club.

Maximum-liability institutions, by contrast, usually have fairly wide-ranging programs, and they take responsibility for whatever their members genuinely need, no matter whether that need was anticipated in advance or not. Israeli kibbutzim are maximum-liability institutions, but such institutions are a rarity in America. Because a maximum-liability institution has the right to make unlimited demands on its members (hence the term *maximum liability*), members of these institutions need to have much in common—shared values, ideals, tastes, and lifestyles. So maximum-liability institutions tend toward homogeneity.

Institutions range from minimum- to maximum-liability. Full, strong communities fall near the maximum end of the spectrum. While it is possible to imagine a community that hasn't institutionalized itself through rules or agreements about decision-making and governance (the chaos of *Gilligan's Island* might qualify), I have never heard of such a community. It doesn't take long before leaders and rules emerge—we are tribal after all. Communities institutionalize in order to stabilize.

Some people consider *institution* a dirty word. When they hear the word *institution,* they think of something big, slow, bureaucratic, expensive, and difficult to change. I dislike those kinds of institutions too. But institutions don't have to be like that. Institutions get that way when they overinstitutionalize. An effective institution is one that can quickly change to meet changing conditions in the larger world and among the people it serves.

Having too many rules or making it too cumbersome to change them is destructive to institutions—it's self-defeating. That's one sure way to ruin a community. A community can only be sustained by an institutional structure strong enough to get things done and light enough for the community to bear.

MEETING MEMBERS' NEEDS

Communities attempt to meet their members' needs in different ways. In America, the marketplace provides an array of goods (consumer items of every description, for example), and governments at every level provide services (education, public safety, defense, and the like). Some communes in the United States have attempted to offer at least some of these goods and services for their members. While communes have many attractions (along with many challenges and complications), that is not what I am talking about here.

Instead, I want to explore the possibility of creating communities within our contemporary social fabric, communities that fit into the overall structure of people's existing lives, if they are willing to change their priorities just a bit. Libertarians would say that there is no need for such communities: Individuals guide their own lives. Socialists might object to this notion of community by saying that in a capitalist economy, even one with as many social welfare programs as the United States, real community is impossible. I reject those two extreme positions. While we might not be able to achieve full maximum-liability communities, I believe that we can come much closer than most people's current experience would suggest.

Since a major purpose of communities is to meet their members' needs, it is important to ask which needs American society often fails to fulfill. As noted above, some of these needs stem from the loneliness people feel. In response to that loneliness, they may be looking for a sense of belonging in a larger group, help in finding a life partner (I suspect I would hate singles bars, too), or both. People seek safety and continuity, ways for their lives to make a difference and ways for them to make a meaningful contribution in a world where it is very hard to leave a mark. Some human needs have their roots in the desire for personal growth—acquiring new skills, increased self-insight, education, or exposure to culture. Some people are looking for fun, joy, and easy laughter. Others are engaged in a spiritual search. Some want to live with people who have shared values and lifestyles or to work on projects with like-minded people. Contemporary synagogues contain people with all these needs, and synagogues at their best meet most of those needs.

Not all these needs must be fulfilled by one community. Admittedly, it's hard to play string quartets by yourself. But a community with a finite number of members might not be able to meet that need. You might have to join the amateur orchestra if you wanted to make symphonic music with other people.

A community can only thrive if it conducts an ongoing conversation about which of these needs the community can reasonably meet. Every group has limited resources. But since a community should respond to as many of its members' needs as possible, I would hope that community leaders would make this a major goal.

ABOUT RITUALS

Some secret societies have special handshakes. Fraternal societies often have induction ceremonies and pledges of allegiance. Gang members wear "colors." Jews recite *Kiddush* (the sanctification over wine) as part of Friday night services. No group can exist without rituals. These usually reflect the boundaries and values of a group, which is critical if the group is to last. Communities have rituals whether they mean to or not.

Rituals have many other functions as well. Good rituals bind the people who share them together. Rituals concretize moments of transition and reinforce people's shared values. And at their best, rituals transcend themselves to point toward ultimate meaning. Rituals that accomplish that are not easy to invent. Of course, one of the functions of religion in human life is to shape our lives through ritual, imbuing our lives with structure and meaning.

One major form of community is the congregation. The rituals of the congregation, and the theology and ideology they express, can create community unity. Examples drawn from Jewish life include *brit mila* (ritual circumcision), *Kol Nidre*, and wearing a tallit (prayer shawl) at morning services. Since beliefs and values are integral to community life, it is extremely helpful if members have at least a measure of agreement about them.

Part of what makes life-cycle occasions like weddings, baby namings, and bar/bat mitzvah and confirmation ceremonies joyful is the community with which we share them. Part of what strengthens us during times of grief and divorce is the support we feel from community. Our communities become central to our lives if we draw comfort from the ritual, agree about its meaning, and have a shared life that goes far beyond the moment.

In every life-cycle moment we can reinforce our way of life if its practices, values, and beliefs are symbolized in the rituals we perform. Breaking a glass at a wedding, for example, strengthens our awareness of the world's brokenness and reminds us of our obligation to repair it. If the community witnessing the ritual affirms the ritual not just as something they are happy for us to do but as something we truly *share* with them, then everyone present gains strength for our commitments that can only come from community.

A synagogue makes a strong base for a community because within it members can experience deeply shared ritual moments—weddings, b'nai mitzvah ceremonies, baby namings, and the like. Each one of these strengthens the life of the community by adding to our shared memories and emotional connections, and by reinforcing the community's values and commitments. At best, this process reinforces itself: Our community supports how we live our lives, and our way of life—expressed through community participation, including ritual—strengthens our community. We need each other not only for emotional support, but for moral support as well. When life-cycle ritual punctuates the life of a community bound together by shared beliefs and practices, it not only reinforces the family at the center of the ritual, it also reinforces the meaning in the lives of each community member, as it binds the community together.

For community to work this way, its members must have a shared ritual. Over fifty years ago, the brilliant theologian Rabbi Mordecai Kaplan suggested that American society depends on its own shared rituals—Thanksgiving, the Fourth of July, Labor Day, Memorial Day, singing "The

Star-Spangled Banner" at the ballpark, and so on. I agree. But that kind of ritual is not intense enough or repeated often enough to support a complete set of beliefs and values. The level of intensity needed to infuse a sense of purpose in life is much more likely to be found in a religious community.

TAKING RESPONSIBILITY

One day while on a trip to Israel, my ten-year-old son saw a fire burning in the field across the street from where we were staying in Jerusalem. When we walked over to take a look, it was clear that we could keep it from spreading, so the two of us started stomping it out. A half-dozen ragged-looking kids happened by and began feeding the fire for fun. Without thinking about it, I yelled at them, chased them away, and soon had the fire out. Afterward, I realized that those kids were big enough to have attacked and really hurt me. In addition, they lived in Israel, and I didn't. Why had I done it? Because in some way I feel responsible for that land and the behavior of its citizens. My son and I did something together that mattered. I hope my son learned something about taking responsibility, and that maybe the kids bent on spreading the fire learned something about citizenship too.

One of modern society's ills is that we have lost the ability to make mutual demands on each other, to do what Leviticus calls *tokheha*: "Thou shalt surely reprove." It takes courage to tell other people that what they are doing is wrong. Whether it is seeing someone carry glass onto the deck of the community pool or watching a punk bully a kid in a train station, our natural tendency is to mind our own business. That's individualism at work. At least within our community, we need to take the commandment to reprove seriously. If we don't help each other live up to our responsibilities and our community's standards, those responsibilities and standards will dissolve before us, and our community along with it. Caring about community means taking responsibility and risking relationships in order to make the community work.

There is a tale about a rabbi who said to one of his less scrupulous congregants, "I wish God were as powerful as people."

The man responded, "What do you mean, rabbi? God is certainly more powerful than people."

The rabbi continued, "You wouldn't steal when there is anyone watching for fear of the consequences. But God is always watching, and you steal with no fear of the consequences!" It is important for others to know we are watching and that there will be consequences to their actions.

As I learned in Jerusalem, once the pattern of taking responsibility and offering *tokheha* is ingrained, we carry it with us when we leave our home communities. When enough of us are doing it, that can have an impact on the larger society as well. But first we need home communities where we will get support for doing *tokheha*. Teaching, learning, and acting on our values and virtues together give us a strength we can never have by ourselves.

Shared Culture

Raised in Salt Lake City, I had many opportunities to experience Mormon culture. One thing that always impressed me was the way talents and skills were honored as part of Mormon life. Singing, playing musical instruments, writing and reciting poetry, drama, dance—they are all seen as God's gifts to be employed in celebrating the Divine. For people active in the Mormon church, there is constant reinforcement for developing their talents and appreciating the talent and achievement of others.

Artistic and cultural expression enhances shared community life. Painters, poets, musicians, and other artists celebrate and reflect on life through their work, and those who appreciate it gain insight, understanding, and experience that augment their lives. In this way, artistic expression enriches both individuals and the community as a whole. A community devoid of cultural expression is a poor place indeed!

For Jews, cultural interchange inevitably involves the study of sacred texts—Torah in the broad sense of Bible, rabbinic texts, and writings through the present day. Such study, like all cultural expression, deepens, critiques, and expands culture, all at the same time. It brings together ancient and contemporary voices, as it asks what has transcendent meaning and what is of transitory importance. Insofar as we add new ideas, values, stories, and images to the ongoing conversation, this process enriches our culture by contributing new threads to its rich weave.

Culture is always evolving—social, scientific, political, and economic forces guarantee that. As Edgar Schein, social scientist and organizational consultant, has pointed out, every organization and every community has its own culture: The question is not whether there will be a culture but what kind of culture it will be. When we look at culture with a critical eye, we gain a measure of control over how our community's culture will evolve: By consciously creating dialogue, we can try out alternatives to practices that aren't working, and we can reach a consensus to discard the practices we have inherited that are no longer working.

Through dialogue, new values can be added to culture. I am grateful for some of the values that have changed life in my Jewish community over the years, including the embrace of equality for women, acceptance of diverse family models, commitment to democratic governance, and empowerment of all members of the community. These new values—which in my life are fused with older ones like social justice, holiness, learning, and mercy—have created a warm, inclusive, safe community where decision-making and leadership roles are shared. As a result, no one bears too great a burden for building the community, and no one is free of responsibility for it either.

2

A COMMITMENT TO CARING

Not all congregations are communities. If most congregants don't know each other on a first-name basis, they don't have a community in the strong sense of the term. If you would not feel comfortable asking virtually any parent of your children's religious school classmates to give your children a ride home while you made a hospital visit, you do not yet have a community.

One of the most striking examples of American society's atomism is that no one is allowed to discipline anybody else's children. In a true community, everybody feels at least a little responsibility for every one of the kids. I know we're building a community when my kids are nowhere to be seen and I take it on myself to say to two kids playing on the front lawn of the synagogue, "Alex, you're playing too loudly with Susan. Quiet down a little."

One of the reasons that a congregation can become a community with relative ease is that everyone shares a core commitment to values and beliefs, meaning that everyone is committed to a purpose beyond simple self-satisfaction. And religious language allows us to talk about moral obligation and social commitment more easily than we can in other contexts. Every denomination and religious movement expresses it somewhat differently, but all congregations seek to help members answer the question, "What does God want from us?" Responding to this question through prayer and social action lies at the heart of religious living.

That places a special burden on the clergy and the congregation's lay leadership. It is not enough to offer worship services and Sunday school classes, perform weddings and funerals, pay salaries and maintain the building. If the congregation is to bring its moral vision to life in a society focused on self-gratification, the congregation must create a community that encourages its members to live out its message.

FINDING A PLACE IN COMMUNITY

In my minyan, the prayer group where I worship on Shabbat and the holidays, we were studying together when someone congratulated the group on how supportive it was of its members. This prompted a lesbian in the group to say that she did not feel fully supported because of some people's use of sexist language. Then a single person said she didn't feel supported because she felt lonely among all the couples. Then one of the married people said he didn't feel supported because the group didn't appreciate the enormous amount of work it takes to sustain a successful marriage. Then one of the parents talked about how hard it is to handle a job and children, and how unreasonable it is for single people to expect families to take the primary responsibility for hospitality. She asked why the singles didn't take more responsibility for the community's children. By then all of us realized that none of us felt appreciated enough.

For me that was a Eureka moment. Suddenly, I realized how the isolation of family units—a natural byproduct of the American commitment to autonomy—placed a huge burden on everyone. Beset by pressures imposed by work and school commitments and raised personal expectations, and with the constant message to "do your own thing," people feel embattled no matter what their family structure. "If you have a fight with your wife, consider a divorce." "If the guy you're dating isn't terrific in every way, stop seeing him."

My Eureka moment showed me the burden that a Jewish community needs to take on to make up for what American society can't and won't do. Community life needs to offer the affection and support that is normally provided by extended family members living in close proximity.

While a congregation can never fully replace a loving extended family, it can replicate the supportive familial environment by using inclusive language that honors the many kinds of family constellations. Congregations can also form small groups within the community where people offer their best efforts and feel appreciated for who they are. For example, congregations can teach parenting skills and provide respite for mothers with young children, as Congregation Beth El Tzedeck does in Indianapolis. Congregations can host Friday night dinners for singles at a nominal cost so they can socialize in a nonpressured atmosphere and also feel cared for and appreciated. These kinds of activities bring people together in a way that builds new relationships. Each community will generate its own list of things its members need. By doing things together, by helping others and being helped, people become part of the web of belonging.

PAYING FOR FRIENDSHIP

After giving a lecture a few years ago, I was chatting with a woman at a reception about how busy her life was. She was describing what made her life feel overloaded and mentioned that she had been going to a therapist every week for thirteen years. I responded sympathetically that she must have had some major issues to resolve. "Oh no," she replied, "I just go there to talk things over with someone I know I can really trust."

In recent years there has been a burgeoning of psychiatrists, psychologists, and other kinds of mental health professionals. I often refer people to therapy because therapists are professionals who have special skills and resources that can have an enormously positive impact on people's lives. Some who seek out these services, however, mistake the professional client-therapist relationship for a personal friendship. These two types of relationships are unique, and serve different purposes in our lives.

Friends share our lives in an ongoing way. We trust them because we know they will still be there for us after we tell them about our struggles and concerns, and we feel good about ourselves knowing that our friends care about us in that way. We expect certain things from our friends— patience, understanding, and support—and our friends expect the same from us. This reciprocity can be demanding, but it is central to building healthy relationships—deep friendships that nurture us, give us ongoing support, and bring us joy.

On the other hand, while therapists typically show concern and caring, they—unlike friends—cannot demand the same from you. There are many times in our lives when we need the help of a professional with specialized expertise, and should seek one out. But we should not substitute the work we do in therapy for the hard work of building close, reciprocal friendships in our daily lives.

Various types of support groups within the community blend elements of both, providing us with help and accountability while also nurturing personal friendships. A community might have a women's group, a parenting group, twelve-step groups (such as Alcoholics Anonymous), prayer groups, study groups, and so on. The bonds formed in these groups are reinforced when we see the same people in other community activities. This moves the relationships built within the support group out into more daily activities, toward friendship.

Abraham Maslow described a hierarchy of human needs beginning with those things necessary for survival—food and shelter—and, for those with the time and energy, culminating in meaning. He pointed out that until we fulfill one need, our attention does not focus on the next. Not long ago, the struggle for food and shelter predominated, as it still does for many people in the world today. Our parents, grandparents, and great-grandparents felt enormous satisfaction in providing food and shelter for their families. Most of us in contemporary Western society have met our basic needs—food and safety—and so we are seeking those things at the top of Maslow's heirarchy; we are searching for meaning. As an Israeli tour guide put it to me recently, "I don't just want bill-payer work. I want my life to mean something." Since we are tribal creatures, much of the meaning in our lives comes from commitment to caring community.

FRIENDSHIP IN ACTION

In a suburban congregation on Long Island some years ago, a woman with cancer had to go to the hospital frequently for chemotherapy, and it left her too weak to drive home. The congregation's members recognized that their help was needed, and they organized a rotation of volunteer drivers. This meant a significant car ride for the volunteer, plus keeping the woman company while she waited in the hospital. It was a remarkable undertaking. Not only did personal bonds develop between driver and patient and among the drivers who shared this powerful experience, but it gave the drivers a new pride in their ability to make a difference for others and new insight into what community is about. And because everybody realized that the community would do the same for them if the need arose, this project engendered new trust in their congregation and greater attachment to it.

Among the services a community could provide for its members are these:

- Carpooling to transport the kids of parents who are ill
- Providing meals for the bereaved
- Visiting the sick and the homebound
- Including recently divorced people in social activities
- Helping parents with newborns
- Notifying the community of major life-cycle news—both good and bad
- Networking to ensure that no one is left alone for holiday meals

- Giving rides to the elderly for meetings and shopping
- Using connections within the congregation to help unemployed members find meaningful work

Every community can easily generate its own list of mutual-support activities. Community leaders usually have friends who meet these needs for them. But people on the periphery—those new to the community and those who are a bit more shy—often fall by the wayside. The community should be organized so we care for everybody.

Jews call helping others and caring about their concerns *gemilut ḥasadim*. *Ḥasadim* comes from the biblical word *ḥesed*, which is often translated as lovingkindness. It describes God's loving, dependable action that goes beyond what justice requires, so *ḥesed* may be translated more accurately as caring, covenantal commitment. Inside a community, we are all called upon to perform acts of *ḥesed* because this practice fills vital needs in people's lives and it builds trust and interdependence.

At first, doing these deeds may feel awkward, but you quickly discover how gratifying it is. Remember the song about how whistling a happy tune keeps you from being afraid? *Acting* like a caring person helps you *become* a caring person. You find that performing deeds of *ḥesed* helps you care about the people you're aiding. When we act as if we are loving, we often end up feeling that way. Thus a system of covenantal, caring, committed action not only strengthens the community, it also helps us grow in commitment and spiritual understanding.

SHARED LIVING

One Saturday morning after services I walked up to a visitor to my minyan and introduced myself. Brimming with enthusiasm, he told me how much he appreciated the intensity of feeling, the powerful singing, and the openness of discussion in this dynamic group. He said that he had been looking for something like this for years, that he would give anything to be part of such a group. It turned out that he lived in the neighborhood, so I told him that the minyan was open to everyone, and he was welcome to come as often as he liked. I explained that everything was done by volunteers, and that after he had been around for a while he would master the melodies, learn enough to follow the Torah (scriptural) discussion, and eventually volunteer to do some of the work of the group. I was disappointed, but not surprised, when he did not come back in subsequent weeks.

I suspect that if he had been able to send someone else to do the learning and pay for somebody else to do the work, if the group were less intimate so that it would be easier to slip in and out unnoticed, he would have joined the minyan. Ironically, what he appreciated most about the group—our intensity of feeling, our shared competence, and our common language of discourse—are products of the mutual commitment that he wanted to avoid.

Many large congregations whose prayers are led entirely by paid professionals worship in ways their congregants find deeply meaningful. Their ministers and rabbis, priests and cantors, choir directors and organists have created cathedral-like spiritual experiences that work for the relatively passive people in the pews because of their beauty, spirituality, and grandeur. Such experiences have great power, but they don't build participatory community, which depends on committed, competent participation.

Community would be more attractive to many people if somebody else did it for them. But it doesn't work that way. The community is mine only if I act like a member of it. The more activities I do in the community, the more interpersonal connections I share, making each activity all the more meaningful. In a voluntary community, where people can leave any time they like, people will stay if they usually get more out of it than they put in. I certainly do: Through my community, I savor friendships, celebrations, insights, spiritual renewal, opportunities to be helpful to others, and I receive support for my family and myself, as well as—dare I say it—meaning for my life.

LOOKING BEYOND OURSELVES

In several books, sociologist Robert Bellah argues that instead of forming communities, people form lifestyle enclaves, such as country clubs and suburbs, that are composed of people with similar backgrounds, educations, ages, political views, and interests. What characterizes a lifestyle enclave is its homogeneity. When you can't pay your dues, you leave the country club. When your kids are grown, you sell your four-bedroom house in the suburbs with the basketball hoop in the driveway. What differentiates a community from a lifestyle enclave, he argues, is that community members' commitments run deeper and the diversity of the members is much greater.

Some of the things I've already talked about (like mutual help) move lifestyle enclaves toward community. But because the kind of community I've been describing functions as a subgroup in a larger society, it can easily take on some of the more pernicious aspects of a lifestyle enclave—self-satisfaction and insularity. For a community to realize its full potential, it must not only feel good, it must act accordingly.

A community must be concerned with the larger society, learning from the outside world and interacting with it in a variety of ways. We need to recognize that obligations flow both from *hesed,* caring covenantal commitment, and from the community's place in the larger society. Since the community functions as home base for its members, the community has a unique opportunity to help its members organize to improve their world. This may take the form of raising funds for worthy causes beyond the boundaries of the community, building houses for Habitat for Humanity, working with the League of Women Voters to educate and motivate voters, volunteering for the local Boys' Club or homeless shelter, working on environmental issues, gathering food for a soup kitchen, or hundreds of other such projects.

Just as an individual seeks meaning when other more pressing needs are met, a caring community seeks a meaningful role in the world once initial concerns about its survival are overcome. Belonging to a community that helps the world beyond itself gives added meaning to my life. And when communities band together to tackle larger projects, the larger social order can begin to be reshaped.

SHARING THE DREAM

In many ways, the model of congregational community I'm sketching has little in common with contemporary American society. So, for many of us, it may take a leap of imagination to see ourselves in such a community.

For those of us who have found or forged this kind of strong community, we too need imagination and support to sustain our commitment. We gain that support in myriad ways: from the feelings we get when we do good things and maintain strong friendships; from the written and spoken messages we receive endorsing our vision, values, and beliefs; from an open acknowledgment of how hard this is to do.

Another way we sustain our commitment to community is by recognizing the virtues we need to be good community members. The philosopher Alasdair MacIntyre has written that, in capitalist society, we constantly think in terms of *extrinsic* goods, things that money can buy. For a community to work, we need to accord full value to *intrinsic* goods—things inside ourselves that are valuable and that often take considerable commitment and energy to nurture and develop. Money-driven systems tend to undervalue these goods because they cannot be bought and sold.

Consider virtues, which are extremely undervalued in contemporary Western society and of critical importance in maintaining community. Among the virtues significant to the kind of community described in this book are forbearance, honesty, gentleness, responsibility, sensitivity to others, and generosity. We need to talk openly about the values and virtues to which we aspire, teach them in our educational programming, and reinforce them in adults and children alike. This character education helps people to better understand what it takes for community to work, and it clarifies what the community expects of them.

We can only create and maintain community if we share both the dream and the discipline to work for its realization. Out of that synergy come many unexpected benefits.

3

BUILDING COMMUNITY

I often think about Dr. Seuss's elephant, the one who announced,

> I meant what I said, and I said what I meant,
> An elephant's faithful one hundred percent!

I try to emulate that elephant, yet sometimes I fall short. When that happens, I pick myself up and try again. The gap between rhetoric and practice is painful, even if it's narrow. There are three ways of dealing with that.

First, we can lower our expectations until any conduct is deemed acceptable. "What do you expect from kids who come from homes like that? It's silly to expect them to do homework or pay attention in class" go the rationalizations.

Second, we can retain the rhetoric and turn a blind eye when people's conduct doesn't match it. For example, I once heard a district attorney whose assistants plea bargain nearly every case tell an audience, "We prosecute every offense to the full extent of the law." This method requires self-deception or willful hypocrisy. When leaders take this approach, they encourage cynicism and contempt.

Third, we can struggle in our daily lives to narrow the gap between rhetoric and practice. That is an unattractive option because it involves an awful lot of work, but I'd rather raise my conduct than lower my rhetoric. That's where community integrity comes from.

It's human nature to conserve energy, probably dating back to winters when food was scarce and those who did too much inessential activity ran out of food and starved to death. It saves a lot of energy to lower community standards. But the cost in quality of life is enormous. Lately, it has cost us the ability to feel safe walking at night on city streets, cleanliness on our playgrounds, and the standards in some public schools.

Most people in our society don't have to worry about starving, even if they expend a lot of extra energy this winter. But they do need to worry about how hypocrisy or lowered community standards will affect their lives. In that light, a little extra work to keep up community standards doesn't seem like such a bad trade-off. While pushing American society to maintain high community standards may be difficult, we can effect change for the better within our Jewish community because of our shared commitment to upholding high standards. By signaling what each member of the community can do to promote the common good, we make everyone part of the same mission.

Getting Started

When people talk to me about starting a new congregation, they are almost always worried about whether they will attract members quickly enough to make the congregation viable. Members are needed to work, to attend community activities, and to establish financial stability. Organizers don't want to discourage anybody from signing up who might be able to help. So they are tempted to solicit new members in the most neutral language possible so as not to turn anyone away.

I usually ask them why they want to undertake the enormous task of starting a new congregation. It inevitably turns out that they have needs and dreams they cannot fulfill without it. What I tell them is that the culture of the community begins to form from the time the first conversations about it take place. After the first few group meetings, things are decidedly less fluid. If we don't articulate a clear vision for our congregational community at the outset, we will have established an organization that tries to be all things to all people. If we want to create a democratic, participatory community that shares certain beliefs and values, then we need to voice that vision from the beginning, inquire about the visions of others who are thinking about joining, develop a common vision with which everyone is comfortable, and thereby move toward creating the kind of community we want. That might well mean adopting a particular ideological label. Mine, for example, would be a Reconstructionist Jewish community. If such an ideological commitment is not present at the outset, community leaders will later have to undertake a substantial process of education and consensus-building, a difficult process that may divide and undermine the entire community.

Seeking an early consensus around a vision may hamper growth in the beginning. Some people reject egalitarian standards or a democratic process when it comes to determining congregational ritual. Others can't imagine a community without them. Building consensus around a vision not only eliminates much painful dissension down the road, but it also empowers people, helping them feel ownership in the group and work on its behalf because their vision is incorporated in the community vision. That vision should lay the groundwork for a statement of beliefs and values as well as a program of cultural, religious, educational, and social justice programs the community will undertake. People who dream find time and energy they didn't know they had to make their dreams a reality.

Restating the dream and modifying it based on experience and the changing nature of the community will keep the dream alive for everyone. Part of what makes us human is that we don't just belong to the world that is. We hope for a world that can yet come to be. By dreaming and sharing our visions, we create a community of hope.

Sending Signals

One of my seminary students, Bonnie Leavy, had been a marketing executive in her former life. She taught me that I could not necessarily reach or move people simply by telling them what was important to me. I had to show them why it would fulfill their needs or help them put their values into action. Only then would it become important to them. "What's in it for me?" is a legitimate and important question. People won't join a community or remain in it if it doesn't meet their needs in some way.

We need to show people what's in it for them when we first sit down with them. But, more than that, we need to signal what needs we're hoping to fulfill when we first approach them. Do we convey the same message in every advertisement? every brochure? every handout? Do we reinforce it by what we say in public, by how we run our meetings, by how we answer the phone?

A community must care about individuals. If I am intrigued by an advertisement for a community activity, I have to overcome my inertia and work up the nerve to make a phone call for more information. If the person who answers the phone is short-tempered or arrogant, or promises a return call or a mailing that never comes, that might well turn me off completely. I end up feeling wounded or frustrated—the notion that this is a caring community seems like empty rhetoric, and I will probably never call again.

We need to send consistent signals about what makes our community special or distinctive, what's in it for those of us who are already members, and what prospective members can expect to gain by affiliating with us. If we believe in participatory prayer, for example, we need to regularly offer training so that new people can master the skills needed for full participation.

Living by Our Rhetoric

Recently, I went to a board meeting where people insulted each other, did not listen when those with whom they disagreed spoke up, and behaved disrespectfully to the people running the meeting. It was painful just to be in the room. As we were leaving, somebody who had found it appalling said to me, "After this, I'm not coming to another board meeting for a while." The bad had driven out the good. Ironically, one of the meeting's discussions had been about why the congregation's members did not feel more committed to the congregational community!

Clearly, this board had lost track of its own values.

Boards and committees need to reflect the community's rhetoric and values, or the community as a whole will soon fail to live up to them.

How can we ensure that the community stays true to its core values and beliefs? Periodically restating our dreams, studying our mission statements, and examining how our beliefs and values play out within every decision-making group in the community certainly help. Otherwise, people don't internalize and apply the group's commitments. But aren't we just too busy for that? Are we like the man who was late for a meeting and drove at breakneck speed in the wrong direction because he didn't have time to pull over and look at the map? We can only make good decisions about how to get somewhere when we agree about where we are and where we're going.

It isn't enough to make good decisions for good reasons. The way we make decisions matters too. The board I described at the beginning of this section had lost track of its commitment to the notion that every human being has infinite worth. A rabbinic statement in the Talmud (Bava Metzia 586) has it that our cheeks turn red when somebody embarrasses us as a reminder that humiliating people is like spilling their blood. Not only had some individuals disregarded that dictum, nobody else had stepped in to remind them. In retrospect, I realized that I too had failed by not speaking out then and there against what was going on.

Boards and committees need to pray together or study together or talk about the way they treat each other. They need to do it often in ways that remind them that community building can only happen when we recognize the face of God in every person with whom we work. A community that values, respects, and therefore listens to every individual who is part of the decision-making process will naturally make decisions that genuinely consider the individuals in the community.

One way to reinforce good community values is to teach them in an organized fashion, such as through *divrey Torah*, short teachings that can open every meeting or gathering. For this to be effective, planning must focus on the values and themes to be covered over time. Coupled with reminders about proper conduct from meeting chairs, this can change the tone and content of meetings significantly. The process of decision making enables us to find out what the community is really about. For the values of the community to come to the fore, they have to be studied, internalized, and then articulated—both verbally and in writing. That is a challenge to every person who cares about community.

A CONTRADICTION IN TERMS?

Since America is a rights-oriented society, creating a community here means creating *voluntary* community. In some ways that is a contradiction in terms. Think what a mess things would be if people could choose whether or not they would be bound by the laws of the countries in which they live. Of course, if you're an American, you can choose whether to stay here or not. If you want to, you can leave America forever.

That is how choosing community works. You can choose to come or go, so we call it voluntary. But as long as you stay, you are bound by the rules of the community. Now if we don't want everybody to leave, we need to figure out ways to make the burden of community membership light enough so that we gain more by membership than we lose.

But if we make membership requirements nothing more than a matter of financial responsibility, we'll end up with a lifestyle enclave rather than a community. So how can we resolve these conflicting demands?

Orthodox Jews live in close proximity to one another because they do not ride on the Sabbath, and they need each other to make up a minyan. Since they consider themselves bound by commandments that require many shared institutions to fulfill, they create these institutions within their community. Their voluntary commitment to observing commandments gives rise to a strong community. Some might say that the Orthodox don't do it voluntarily; after all, they inherited the commandments. But as many formerly observant Jews have shown, it is possible to change personal practice and leave that community. In America, all religious practice is voluntary. Anyone who identifies with any religious belief, any religious or ethnic community, does so voluntarily.

While I personally disagree with certain aspects of the Orthodox community's beliefs and practices, I envy its intense sense of community. Orthodox Jews recognize how much they have to gain by living together in their community, doing what they believe God wants—something they couldn't do any other way.

For those of us outside the Orthodox world, community building is not so simple. Belonging to a community is a difficult choice. If initial demands on us are too high, or if we don't believe we'll benefit almost immediately, we won't join. Commandments don't dictate our involvement. That creates the most difficult conundrum communities contemplate: How do we elicit enough commitment from each member while including enough people?

CREATING PARTICIPATION

Several strategies have emerged in response to this dilemma. Some communities impose higher requirements to start with and accept lower membership. One ancient model of voluntary community is the monastery or nunnery. Full membership in these orders carries substantial responsibility and requires a great deal of discipline.

Thirty years ago I was the rabbi of a congregation that had a point system. Every kind of work for the congregation was assigned a certain number of points, and every adult had to earn one hundred points each year. To everybody's surprise, most people had little trouble earning far more than one hundred points, which was a great morale booster. But the system also scared away potential members who would have added much to the community. That included people who would have had no trouble fulfilling the requirement once they took the time to get to know the community.

One way of lowering the barrier is for new members to have less responsibility for an initial period. This approach may still be viewed as too restrictive by some, but it does have the virtue of guaranteeing that everyone in the community is doing their fair share. This two-tiered method both reduces the burden on the most committed and signals to them that everyone is committed to the work of the group, a significant morale builder for hardworking leaders.

An alternative to requiring each member to perform substantial volunteer service is to avoid specifying any work or participation obligation as a requirement. Once individuals are benefiting from the work of the community, then they are asked to volunteer. At first they are asked to undertake small tasks that introduce them to other community members. As they become familiar with the community and gain more gratification from the work, they are asked to take on larger and more complex tasks.

A hybrid approach would impose requirements for participation in certain community activities. For example: "If you want your kids to have the retreat experience, you must commit yourself to coming and participating fully as well." "Since this is a complicated project, you must agree to come to every session." Or even, "Only those who attend the study sessions will be allowed to vote on the community's policy." But while this may help to create pockets of greater commitment and enthusiasm near the center of the community, it does not solve the problems at the periphery.

In many congregations, the core of the congregational community is composed of intensely involved people who participate heavily both in the work and in the programs of the congregation. As a result, they have strong interpersonal connections and a powerful sense of community. These connections and community support the core group's commitment.

The opposite is true among inactive members. They hardly participate in the work or activities of the congregation; their interpersonal connections in the congregation are weak, and they may feel alienated from the community. They may dimly perceive a friendship network operating at the core of the congregation, but from the periphery it is likely to appear more like a clique than a community. The longer they languish on the periphery, the less likely they are to be drawn toward the center. From their vantage point, the congregation may not only fail to be a community, it may fail to be even a lifestyle enclave. Rather, they view it as an uninteresting yet necessary affiliation for giving their children exposure to religious teachings and traditions, or for holding life-cycle events. Otherwise, they remain unconnected.

What's more, the people on the periphery have little opportunity to absorb the congregation's mission or culture. They do not experience the interpersonal intimacy that forms a bridge into and out of religious experience. Nonetheless, these alienated and uninvolved people are members of the congregation. The experience is bad for them, and their alienation undermines the congregation's attempt to function as a community by sapping it of energy, unity, intensity, and clarity of purpose.

So how can a voluntary community maintain its focus and drive without strong participation requirements? By doing all it can to avoid leaving people on the periphery.

- Phone trees need to reach out to every member, going in one direction to carry news of congregational programs and in the other to carry hopes, criticisms, and suggestions.
- Buddy systems should pair activists with new members and those on the periphery, inviting them to meals, bringing them to congregational activities, explaining how things work, introducing them to other people, gently cultivating increased knowledge, skill, and participation.
- Volunteer tasks need to be broken down into very small pieces so that those with little time or commitment can start to feel part of the congregation by doing something on its behalf. If possible, these initial tasks should be person-to-person projects that clearly make a difference in the life of the recipient. This gratifies both

parties and forms a bond that draws them more strongly into the congregation. The activities undertaken need to be explained in terms of religious and communal values, beliefs, and norms so that participants see their actions not just as haphazard good deeds but as reflecting aspects of religious tradition and the community's moral commitment.

- Interviews of new members should gather in-depth information about their skills, interests, knowledge levels, hopes, needs. These should be reviewed regularly by the program committees and volunteer coordinators within the congregation.

- Periodic evening gatherings in small groups can give members a chance to offer feedback and to allow leaders to explain community initiatives and learn about people's interests. Chance remarks made under these circumstances can generate some brilliant new projects. These small groups also create interpersonal connections and send the message that every person matters.

These suggestions are far from an exhaustive list. Will they solve the problem? No. But they, and other ideas like them, have the potential to reduce the size and intensity of the problem for the voluntary community by reducing the number and the alienation of people on the periphery.

These changes may encounter substantial resistance. After all, those drifting on the periphery of our communities may still be contributing—through their financial donations, by swelling membership rolls, and by boosting the congregation's public visibility. And their very lack of involvement may allow stronger, more committed leaders to guide the organization without undue interference. Congregations don't want to lose those on the periphery; still, most communities gain strength from active, committed members rather than passive alienated people just coasting along.

How much people feel obligated to reach out to the uninvolved will also determine how interested people are in holding onto the periphery. One Orthodox rabbi told me that he barred nonobservant people from joining his congregation because he didn't want them diluting the community's intense religious atmosphere. By contrast, some Reform congregations have made reaching out to unaffiliated Jews central to their self-understanding.

Whom should we serve? How should we serve them? What should we demand in return? How do we determine the boundaries of our community and the meaning of belonging? These are questions every community must answer for itself, not just once but over and over again.

4

Radiant Centers

In 1984 my friend Carl Sheingold, a sociologist of American Jewry, introduced me to the theory of radiant centers, which since then has figured prominently in my thinking. A radiant center is a person or activity that beams sufficient light and warmth to attract others to it.

What draws us into a community? It could be an enlightening speaker or a wonderful teacher; a soulful choir or the opportunity to learn new rituals in a supportive environment; a gentle counselor or an effective liturgical leader. It could be the caring commitment of a circle of people who provide support during a difficult personal crisis, or a _havurah_ (a small fellowship group). Or dozens of other things.

These activities can move people from the periphery toward the center. In a thriving congregation, there are multiple radiant centers. The congregation's clergy have the time and energy to be involved in only some of them. That means that a successful community cannot be totally centralized. Because the radiant centers do not involve all the same people, they create several centers of congregational life rather than just a single one. They are tools of outreach to those outside the congregation, and they are also ways of creating connection—and feelings of belonging—within the congregational community. They are sources of light and warmth for those who participate in them.

One of the problems with many large congregations today is that little happens to energize and renew core members. They settle into comfortable routines while the community's life gradually grows stale and uninteresting. Since part of the purpose of the congregational community is to provide for the personal growth and spiritual development of its members, and since the core group sets the tone for the congregation at large, the radiant centers are often most needed by those at the center. It is easier for people if no one challenges their ways of thinking and living, but that is a way of living that stunts growth and eventually causes the community to deteriorate.

Radiant centers tap into people's best talents by calling on them to undertake risks and experiments. To make this work, the professional and lay leadership must be willing to relinquish some control. An English professor might be recruited to lead a monthly discussion group on Jewish short stories. A community organizer might join with a teacher to recruit and train tutors for a nearby school. A klezmer band can be pulled together. By infusing new energy and new ideas into the congregation, radiant centers generate excitement, create hope, and achieve religious renewal.

Radiant centers are thus the most important part of inreach, of creating interconnection, a sense of belonging, and meaningful involvement within a community. They motivate and energize the membership; they even have the ability to transform members' lives. The closer people are to one activity of the community, the more likely they are to become committed to other activities and to move toward communal leadership. Once people are involved in one radiant center, they often become involved in others as well, thereby adding immeasurably to the intensity and mutuality of the community.

As radiant centers develop, more people on the periphery bask in their warmth. The more radiant centers there are in a congregation, the more people will be affected and the more they can be sustained as part of the community. Radiant centers bring institutional vibrancy, programmatic change, and religious renewal. Once experiencing them, leaders wonder how they ever lived without them. One rabbi invited a charismatic teacher to conduct a new weekly course after months of hesitation and worry about being upstaged. Several months later the rabbi said to me, "He's doing a great job, and I'm getting the credit for making it possible." When things go well, the whole leadership shines.

Growing Season

In the grocery store not long ago, I saw a mother scold her child for a minor misdeed. Pretty soon she started warming to her subject. She talked louder and moved on to name-calling. Soon she was well into her subject, telling her son that he would never amount to anything. By then she had built to a crescendo, and she concluded by giving the child a hard swat on the bottom. Of course, the child had dissolved into sobs long before the end of the tirade, so I am not certain how much of it he heard. But one thing I am sure of: He understood that in his mother's eyes he didn't amount to much. Now that's a level of motherly expectation that is not too hard to live up to—or, should I say, live down to.

In a much less strident way, many community leaders

do what that mother did. They undermine the sense of self-worth of their followers by holding them up to impossible standards. That little boy was stuck with his mother. But adults don't have to put up with abuse. If they have enough self-respect, they simply walk away, or they work to change the leadership. If they don't have a heavy dollop of self-respect, they feel the way that little boy must have—that somehow they really are unworthy. Leaders without empathy undermine themselves and their congregations, because criticism without compassion sets in motion a self-defeating pattern—the community sinks to the level of the leader's real expectations, attendance wanes at programs and events, and the congregation's self-image crumbles. Now the membership won't even try to replace their leader because they think they deserve what they're getting.

Education professor Christina Ager suggests that students need to hear compliments and encouragement ten times as often as criticism if they are to improve their behavior. Otherwise, they become too discouraged to marshal the resources needed to improve. Adults are no different. A little criticism goes a long way.

People grow with the help of gentle encouragement. They gingerly reach out to others, hoping to receive support. They take on new obligations or try out new skills tentatively and awkwardly, but also with growing hope and strength.

To build community, we must remember to nurture. We need to dream dreams and support new growth.

Seeing Visions

When congregations ask me to visit, it is often because they want help solving a problem—sometimes financial, sometimes programmatic, sometimes factional. The problem that prompted my visit doesn't usually turn out to be the fundamental one. Often there is a dullness or malaise that has settled into the congregation's life. I ask questions like, "Where are you trying to go? What are your hopes for the future?" And it often turns out that their hope for the future is that tomorrow won't be much worse than today—a painfully modest ambition that limits the congregation in myriad ways.

If you expect little and do not work to accomplish anything new, it takes extraordinary good luck to make major progress. But it is almost impossible to stand still. People in close proximity who are not working together for a common purpose end up running around in circles and banging into each other. The only way to keep them from wandering around aimlessly and stepping on each other's toes is to help them discover where they would like to be going. They need to find their own vision.

Some people think that visionaries come up with their far-reaching ideas by carefully studying the world. I don't think so. We all know a great deal about what the world is like; in fact, our knowledge often prevents us from being visionaries. Visionaries are people who close their eyes and dream not about what the world is but about what it could be—and they don't stop at the daydreaming stage. They compare current reality to their dream and set about narrowing the distance between the two, a process that the management guru Russell Ackoff has called closing "the planning gap."

This process can bring about world transformation and community transformation. But an equally critical key to community transformation is individual transformation, for a community is only as strong as its members make it. If a community is to have energy and direction, depth and vision, its members must share those qualities.

How do we develop the capacity for vision in ourselves? Vision grows out of the raised expectations that come from living in a caring community energized by its radiant centers. Vision also comes from learning to dream about ourselves rather than about bigger TVs, faster cars, or nicer houses. Dreaming about myself isn't a simple thing because I have been taught to focus on extrinsic things, things outside myself, rather than intrinsic things, what is happening with my inner life.

Where can dreaming about myself begin? Human nature hasn't changed much in the last ten thousand years. We humans are just as loving and small-minded, violent and gentle, ambitious and wise as ever. We can begin dreaming by listening to the visions and pitfalls charted for us by the visionaries of the past—philosophers, fiction writers, poets, and religious thinkers.

The study of sacred texts prompts us to ask questions about ourselves and the ultimate meaning in our lives. It asks us to take a different kind of look at who we are and what we are capable of doing and becoming. A classical Jewish way to tackle the study of sacred texts is to do it in _hevruta,_ study pairs. By closely reading and discussing the text together, each partner benefits from the other's insights, questions, and answers. Sometimes it's the questions that are the hardest to formulate. This method can be applied to Bible study or to the study of any other kind of text, including rabbinics, commentaries, and contemporary classics.

Through this kind of study we discover more about the holiness in ourselves and about the moral possibilities and pitfalls in human existence. In turn, we develop greater ambition to cultivate our inner lives. We channel that ambition into activities we undertake in solitude—reading, writing, meditation, and dreaming—but its full expression also requires engagement in the community. By turning dreaming into planning, we can transform both ourselves and our community. Most communities suffer from a crisis of lowered expectations. Dreams of inner clarity and depth revitalize us as they offer a creative challenge for the community.

LONELINESS AND SOLITUDE

Growing up in the midst of the Rocky Mountains, I remember well the feeling of struggling up a rocky peak, and the tiredness and the triumph upon reaching the summit. Sitting at the top on a summer day, it was always both sunny and cool because the wind was never still. Looking out over the broad expanse, I could see miles of green forest and meadow, hill and valley. There was wonder there— grandeur and smallness at once, and a sharp perspective on my life in the world.

Those moments were my first taste of solitude. Solitude is very different from loneliness—what we experience when we're sick at home, cut off from friends; or when we're unsure about who to call for a date to the dance; or when we're staring at the clock, knowing that hours of unwanted isolation lie ahead. We are lonely when we don't want to be alone; we are in solitude when we are alone yet exquisitely aware that though we are all alone in some ways, we are also part of something infinitely bigger than our daily lives. There is enormous strength in solitude.

Shared communal life should help us overcome lonely moments. There is no substitute for caring human contact, and communities are the best place to find it. But communal life can only help us deal effectively with our loneliness in the long term if it helps us appreciate solitude, if it helps make us comfortable being a small part of something much larger than ourselves.

The community cannot always be with us; it cannot fulfill our every need. If we demand that of the community, we will overtax it, and it will become a source of frustration and disappointment. When the community is asked for what it cannot give, it must gently but firmly say no for its own sake. Often this turns out to be for the sake of the asker as well. We never develop skill and strength in areas where somebody else always steps in to do those things for us. Part of the community's task is to help people discover their own inner resources and take responsibility for themselves. The religious community should foster in people a greater connection with the Divine so they can find ways to balance community with solitude. A community member who can find comfort in solitude will add strength and perspective to the community, and will draw greater strength from it as well.

There are many paths to solitude. Some find it in prayer, sacred study, or meditation; others cultivate their inner lives in the solitude of nature—on mountaintops, in forests, by the ocean; still others revel in the solitude of practicing a craft or doing artwork. A strong community supports many paths.

A Shabbat morning service might be preceded by a half-hour meditation session. An individualized program of spiritual direction may take advantage of the recent surge in training Jewish spiritual directors. One evening a week the library may be devoted to _hevruta_ study. The possibilities are endless.

GROWING INTO COMMUNITY

Many years ago my friends Arlene and Howard Eisenberg took the phrase "ladder of observance" from the writing of Abraham Joshua Heschel and wrote up ladders of observance for the various Jewish holidays. They suggested to the not-yet-observant that they could climb each holiday ladder one rung at a time, moving upward at their own pace.

Communities have many different ladders, many different paths into greater participation and connection. In a voluntary community we must constantly issue invitations for people to join us in wandering further up the paths. And when the paths diverge, we should encourage people to follow their instincts. It doesn't matter which of the paths to community they are on, as long as they are continuing to make the journey.

Many aspects of community life can work together to support this approach, from using inviting language in every memo, oral announcement, and newsletter, to leaders using active listening so that members will feel encouraged to speak openly what is on their hearts and minds, to finding ways to help a dissatisfied person set out on a new path instead of simply walking away. It is a matter of attitude. In building community, we help everyone to weave ever stronger the fabric of interconnection and commitment.

Every activity that connects people to one another acts as a radiant center. So does an inspiring connection to a teacher or activity. Inreach requires constructing such opportunities and making them accessible. Strong communities contain many such opportunities for cultivating growth and relationships.

5

Becoming a Community Leader

Aminister once had a church filled with dissension. Drained and frustrated, he was considering resigning. He was a good preacher, worship leader, and administrator. His religious faith was unshaken, which is no small thing since everyone's faith is shaken sometimes, but this dissension had crept up in both his previous posts. I asked him how he felt about the members of his church, and a torrent of frustration, anger, and confusion poured out. He felt injured, abused, bored, exploited, undervalued, and undersupported. I told him that he would only be able to stay if he learned to love his congregants more. He later developed a successful noncongregational career elsewhere.

A successful community operates like a substitute tribe or clan. People turn to their leaders for many things—spiritual and moral guidance, solace, organizational direction—but perhaps the most important of these is love. This may take various forms, including a cry for attention, recognition, or acceptance. Some people may only reach out to their leaders during crises like a death or major life changes like marriage. But at some point everyone needs recognition from the heads of the community (if they are to perceive it as *their* community). When those leaders really care, it sets the tone for the whole community.

Love flows outward. As each person is touched by it, that person passes it on to others in countless little ways. Eventually, the whole community benefits. Like a family, a community thrives on love. When love is withheld by a person in authority—a parent or a community leader—all sorts of problems develop, such as interpersonal conflict, jealousy, competition, and soul-sapping ennui. Love expressed by others, while comforting, never makes up for a parent who doesn't love you enough. The ill will in a family bereft of love mirrors the acrimony in the congregation with the unhappy or uncaring minister.

The love of a congregational leader for his or her community members takes many forms: careful listening, a phone call when someone hasn't been around for a while, drawing somebody in by encouraging her to contribute a particular talent or skill, rearranging a schedule to squeeze in a person with a problem. There are many ways to show people you care. We all need to know that our leaders care about us.

That doesn't mean that communities guided by loving leaders will have no problems. Deep disagreements about the direction of a community's programs, its boundaries, its finances, or its management will be painful no matter what, and there is no cure-all for errors, laziness, or incompetence. But even in these cases, caring commitment can lessen the pain and make reconciliation possible.

I have known several rabbis who were not particularly gifted intellects, speakers, programmers, or administrators yet who became deeply beloved by their congregations. When I talk to their congregants, it doesn't take long to find out why: They know their rabbi loves them and will be there for them. They trust that other leaders and teachers in the congregation will make up for the rest, which seems trivial to these congregants in comparison to what their rabbi gives them.

How Much Can I Give?

We all know that leaders get just as tired, frustrated, and angry as anyone else. Sometimes the love they receive from their families soothes and reinvigorates them. Sometimes the demands placed on their families and friends just drain those tanks as well. When your emotional tank is on empty, you can't be sufficiently caring.

I am fortunate that I have deep respect for my colleagues with whom I work at the seminary. Therefore, it is easy for me to act and feel caring toward them. We have grown in strength together. When I am weary or frustrated, they often lift my spirits with their caring. I couldn't have given nearly as much if I didn't have those people—board members, administrators, faculty, and students—giving to me as well.

In accepting caring, the recipient also gives a gift. As part of a community of caring, I am so much stronger than I ever could be alone! When we all give to each other, we draw caring from a well that we are constantly refilling.

In a more supportive, better organized community, this sense of being drained may happen to a leader a little later than in a community in disarray, but, no matter what, leaders sometimes run out of energy. They may focus their negative feelings on a single individual, subgroup, or event, lashing out in subtle or not-so-subtle ways. Sometimes they may be a mass of free-floating rage, directed at everyone and everything.

When leaders deny their feelings, it only makes matters worse. It's tough to repair things if you haven't acknowledged that they are broken. Furthermore, denial can make things much worse because it models dishonesty and hypocrisy.

Leaders need rest and renewal. They need to pace themselves. The tortoise did, after all, cross the finish line first. Leaders also need opportunities to talk about what is bothering them. And often they need expert, impartial advice about how to express themselves in a way that will help rather than hurt both them and their communities. Most of all they need to understand and acknowledge their own limits. What leaders alone cannot accomplish, they can do together with others in their communities.

Dreaming in Full Color

After an absence of eight years, I met with the board of a congregation in the Midwest that I had formerly visited annually. I had led several board workshops and made many friends there over the years, so imagine my surprise when I looked around the room and saw only a couple of familiar faces. When I started to talk with them about what had formerly been familiar themes to the board of this congregation, I suddenly realized that, for this group, this would be entirely new ground. They were bright people, and I didn't mind beginning again. However, it was clear that a significant portion of this community's collective memory had been lost.

Shared community memory is short when leadership and membership keep changing. The next generation doesn't necessarily share the memories of the generation that preceded it. Leaders must state and repeat the community's vision, history, values, beliefs, and norms with great frequency, not only for the sake of new leaders and members but also for the sake of existing members. With busy lives and practical concerns, people tend not to think about the principles on which their lives are based. If they are to be ready when they are really needed, community policies need regular review. That is a lesson that corporations concerned with ethical behavior are now recognizing as well.

But simply repeating the key parts of the message is not enough. To keep it current, the key principles need regular review. The pressure of everyday community concerns makes most leaders reluctant to "waste" time on efforts that produce no tangible results. But renewing the vision and policies of the community is a critical part of keeping the community united and moving forward.

Leaders need to regularly involve the whole community in thinking about its direction. Surveys, town-hall meetings, written reports from committees and boards, and public presentations to the whole community all have a role to play. People need to participate because they will only own the vision if they are a part of it. And no community can fulfill the highest vision of which it is capable without every member's help.

The vision that emerges from everyone's input should not be a gray, lowest-common-denominator thing. If leaders are truly leading, the vision will sparkle with brilliant color, courage, and hope.

CREATING DIALOGUE

When I tell people I believe in democratic community, they often equate it with one of several deeply flawed versions: anarchy, mob rule, a community committed to radical change, a community that does not respect its leaders. Of course, all these are possibilities, but prudent action can prevent the community from sliding into such an unhappy situation.

For a democratic community to thrive, leaders must first put in place decision-making processes that reflect an inclusive approach and recruit members to participate in making decisions. Leaders must also articulate vision, share insights, and encourage informal dialogues that create momentum for the community. In this way leaders facilitate good decision making without playing a neutral role. Only a leader who simultaneously supports democracy and exhibits passion and vision will accomplish this successfully.

Free and open communication is the enemy of any authoritarian system. That is why totalitarian governments inevitably practice vigorous censorship. The enemy of democracy is silence. The more we talk, the more we exchange views, the more we seek dialogue with those with whom we disagree, the more vigorous a democracy is. When leaders try to do things in a top-down way, the energy disappears from the group, because vigorous participation only thrives with two-way communication.

No leader understands or appreciates the diverse experiences of the members of the community without hearing from them directly. Many of the suggestions, fresh ideas, and key criticisms of the status quo come from members themselves. But that only happens if leaders actively encourage dialogue and go out of their way to listen carefully and non-judgmentally when new ideas are expressed.

People who feel their ideas have been taken seriously are much more likely to accept the decisions of their leaders. And people who feel empowered by the way their leaders treat them will work more energetically on behalf of the community. They will also continue to generate new ideas and offer their views in ways that invigorate the community.

Some organizational boards simply rubber-stamp the decisions made by officers of the organization. Leaders who want a free hand bend the board to their will in several ways: leaving little time for discussion at board meetings, engineering board meetings so new ideas or criticisms of the status quo are pounced on and savaged by those supporting business as usual, or rotating those who "make trouble" off the board. These tactics weaken a board, exclude the most energetic and creative future leaders, and fail to confront the need for change.

Inertia in a board tends to dull community life. When new leaders want to change that, they can begin by changing the program and message, but the new way of doing things will not be fully workable until the board again becomes a vigorous group that is open to new ideas, reflects the membership, and has its support.

HONORING SERVICE

People love to be honored for something they are proud to have done well, to bask in the community's appreciation. Recognition by our tribe means a great deal to all of us, whether it be a well-placed comment at a meeting, an inscription on a plaque, a formal presentation in someone's honor, or an event at which the honoree is saluted.

Most people think that we honor someone primarily for the sake of the honoree, but I think the community is the primary beneficiary. Honoring the right kind of person gives the community a chance to reaffirm its values. It gives us a chance to express our gratitude and to contemplate an example of conduct worth emulating.

Showing appreciation to those who serve and lead us has another benefit: It makes service more attractive to others. Anticipated recognition should not be the reason someone performs acts of altruism, but recognition is a way of helping people feel good about their altruistic choices.

Some communities feel reluctant to honor those who serve because they have seen groups that honor people in an insincere or ostentatious way. Some groups only honor those who give large sums of money, or who provide an immediate benefit to the organization. We must recognize the importance of honoring workers. While it is legitimate to honor those who offer substantial financial support, when we don't honor those who deserve it for other reasons, we risk fostering resentment and cynicism that can erode the community from within.

Leaders teach us how to honor others by how they honor those who serve and lead the community. By publicly recognizing and appreciating what others say and do, leaders honor us and encourage us to do the same for others. Communities—and their leaders—reveal a great deal about themselves by who, how, and when they honor.

LEADING RITUAL

People depend on rituals to structure their lives and point out the significance of daily living as well as life's milestones. A community leader therefore automatically functions as a ritual leader. When the leader taps a gavel to mark the beginning or end of a meeting, that is a ritual.

The congregational community's religious rituals will

often blend seamlessly with the rest of its rituals. A Jewish congregation might install its officers in conjunction with a Friday night service or call its new president to the Torah during a Saturday morning service and add a prayer for the president's success in office. In a congregational community, leaders are called on to mesh rituals with political and religious values to form a single harmonized system that reinforces the community's beliefs, values, and practices.

In all communities, leaders must find ways to mark beginnings and endings, successes and failures, comings and goings with rituals that reinforce what the community believes and values. Usually this can be done by utilizing inherited rituals. Occasionally new ones must be invented. For example, when I was to be installed as president of my seminary, I realized that no ceremony for this occasion had been developed for my predecessors. The simple ritual we developed had as its centerpiece the chairman of the board presenting me with a beautiful tallit as a mantle of authority. This worked in part because the tallit already has rich meaning and because the lay leaders confer authority on my seminary's rabbinic leaders.

Rituals for occasions such as recognizing new honorary board members, saluting extraordinary volunteers, or burning a mortgage reinforce values and celebrate milestones. Using ritual well helps to keep the community united.

6

DEALING WITH CONFLICT

One day I asked a group of my students what they thought of when they heard the word *conflict*. They mentioned "argument," "fighting," and "war," among other negative terms. When I suggested that conflict is often a good thing, my students responded with surprise and disbelief. That response goes far toward explaining how many leaders deal with conflict.

If conflict in my community is the nuisance that keeps me, as a leader, from getting what I want, then my reaction will be to suppress, subvert, or circumvent the conflict. While these strategies might avoid conflict for a time, the sources of disagreement will only fester beneath the surface, gathering energy to surface again as other, possibly worse, confrontations. Community requires commitment, which flows in part from taking each other seriously—especially when we disagree. If people feel ignored and do not want to leave the community, either they become passive or they organize an active opposition.

A wise leader recognizes that conflict may be a red flag, signaling that things need to be changed. Has the leadership failed to fully consider the rights and needs of some members of the community or failed to appreciate all the consequences of a particular proposal? Have leaders inadequately communicated why we are proposing something and how it will work or ignored other proposals worthy of consideration? Are we asking one constituency to give up too much?

When conflict occurs in a congregation, it usually becomes heated when people feel that they are not being taken seriously. Everybody wins when we encourage the expression of alternative views while keeping in mind that the issues they raise may benefit everyone. For leaders, that means setting aside the belief that we are the experts who know best, or that for all our work we are entitled to get what 'we want. Leaders must remember that everyone—clergy, volunteer leaders, and lay members—co-owns the community; we are all in this together.

When I am struggling to listen to the opinions of others instead of simply asserting my own vision, I try to keep in mind a rabbinic dictum. Roughly translated, it states: "These and those are the words of the living God." I cannot be certain that I know the divine will. Sometimes I'm not sure my opinion would even qualify as a good guess. And God speaks in many voices. It would be foolish of me not to take every person's heartfelt words as potentially conveying a divine intent. With that in mind, I know I need to listen. When we glean from each comment the key fragments of insight, inspiration, and fact, we can figure out how to move forward together. Guiding us there is the task of leadership.

TEACHING PLURALISM

Two little boys were arguing on a playground. I began to pay attention as their words grew more heated, but I decided I would step in only if it looked like they might come to blows. As I listened, it became apparent that they were brothers. When the argument moved toward its climax, one yelled at the other, "Mom loves me best." "Does not." "Does too." "Does not." "Does too." By then the smaller boy had burst into tears, and the last I saw of them he was running home with the older boy trailing along behind him.

That story reminds me of the dog-food commercial on TV that proclaimed, "My dog's better than your dog, my dog's better than yours, my dog's better 'cause he eats _____, my dog's better than yours." (I won't give the manufacturer the satisfaction of mentioning its name.) "My dog" is a cousin of the ever popular "My dad can beat up your dad."

These scenarios reflect people's insecurities about whether they are loved enough, strong enough, good enough. The issue in these stories is whether Mom loves me enough so that I feel good about myself, whether my dog is healthy and attractive, whether my dad makes me feel safe. When we are not sure about these things, we start looking around and comparing ourselves to other people. These kinds of comparisons are designed to confirm our self-worth, but the process is destructive because the outcome leaves at least some people feeling bad about themselves. Oftentimes, everybody ends up feeling bad.

But there is another way of looking at others, one that involves seeing how and why they do things and studying the results so that we can learn from them and grow, improving ourselves by emulating others. While that makes us stronger in the end, it requires us to acknowledge our weaknesses. We need to feel secure enough about ourselves to recognize where we are weak and feel strong enough to do something about it.

When people who feel secure about themselves get together, they tend to cooperate rather than compete. It doesn't much matter to them whose dog is better, whose dad is stronger, or whom Mom loved more. Feeling secure means that what I have is enough—not necessarily all I might want, but enough. The same is true of communities. Their leaders need to bolster the community's collective ego to the point where it achieves that feeling of security. Such a community exudes strength and attracts people who feel comfortable in stable, noncompetitive environments. It has the courage to face itself honestly and make things still better.

Where do such strength and courage come from? First, Mama and Papa really *do* have to love you enough. In the same way, leaders really *do* have to love the membership enough. Second, members have to *realize* that the leaders love them enough. Leaders must tell them so, in many different ways, to help them internalize the message. Leaders need to make members conscious of how well loved they are. Third, they have to help the members understand that caring and cooperation build community, and that a strong and caring community will most likely provide enough to its members. Not all we might fantasize about having, but enough. If we can just accept that we have enough, then we will be able to stop competing.

Pluralism connotes exactly this sort of acceptance of difference. Every successful community has to accept some differences—differences in abilities, interests, ways of doing things. A democratic, voluntary community has to be pluralistic: The spectrum of views and idiosyncrasies it encompasses has to be wide. Leaders have to set an example by listening and responding to those with different ideas and visions, thereby honoring each individual. By itself, however, that is not enough. The only way pluralism can thrive is if we as a community feel secure. Even if your mom didn't love you enough, our community does. Even if you felt vulnerable out there in the world by yourself, in here we look out for each other.

Leaders must find various ways to say, "Welcome home! Here you will find what you need." Then leaders and members together must ensure that it is so. Only in such a community will commitment to pluralism grow.

THE BIGGER PICTURE

People who play "My dog is bigger" don't just do it in their families and their communities; they also do it at the level of intercommunal and world affairs. Playing out personal pain on a larger stage can result in international tragedy—war, genocide, and so on. On a larger scale it is even more difficult to decide what is "enough." Mature people, communities, and nations do struggle mightily to figure that out in a way that gives everyone what they need. Nobody ever gets everything they want, unless they have minimized their expectations in an extraordinary way.

There is a Jewish tale about a saintly man who goes through a life of desperate deprivation. When he dies and goes to heaven, the heavenly court tells him that, in light of his goodness, any request he makes will be granted, so he asks to be given a fresh, warm roll to eat every day. The court gasps at his simple request and asks if he might want anything else. In trepidation at his own audacity, he adds, "and a bit of butter." Contemporary communities and nations never suffer from that kind of limited expectation for long. But how do we hold onto our valid group ambitions without feeling deprived?

Many communities and nations play the grown-up version of "My dog is bigger." In the most tragic version of this game, "My army is bigger," nations attempt to prove their claim by going to war. But this cycle starts long before we get to that point. When somebody says, "My dog is bigger," it takes enormous strength and will not to respond, "No, *my* dog's bigger." How wonderful to be able to respond, "I love my dog. I'm glad you love your dog too."

When we choose not to emulate the beliefs or practices of another community, we need to know why we prefer our own way. And we need to feel secure enough in who we are that we resist the impulse to tell the other community, "Our dog [our way] is better." Rather, when they ask us to talk about our approach, we will do it in a manner that shows our love and pride. That should be enough.

Such a response exemplifies pluralism. On the larger stage of intercommunal affairs, this kind of response acknowledges that different communities have different beliefs, values, and practices. Naturally, each community feels that its beliefs and practices are best, yet as we learn about each other's practices, we come to understand each other, and this fosters cooperation. Pluralism requires us to recognize others' authenticity. If we really believe that our way is wonderful, we can have faith that others will eventually see the light and learn from us as well.

Intercommunal exchanges, in which we come together in mutual respect and acceptance, allow us to create a community of communities. These communities of communities span the towns and cities of America. Together these communities of communities can teach ethics and civics, provide moral direction, and release enough energy to tackle some of our larger social ills.

That kind of cooperation can happen only if community leaders commit themselves to promoting intercommunal dialogue and addressing larger societal concerns, and incorporate that into their community's vision. Intercommunal pluralism can only work if we find ways to get along with people very different from ourselves.

If a Jewish congregation is not large enough to operate a soup kitchen daily, it might split that task with neighboring Methodist and Catholic churches as well as a nearby Buddhist temple or Muslim mosque. If we are concerned about gun control, a religious lobby that is pandenominational can be very effective. If we need a new neighborhood ball field, or support for additional police patrols, or a myriad other community tasks performed, we can do things in coalition with other organizations that our own community cannot do on its own.

When communities that have deep differences manage to overcome them for the common good, they have forged a vibrant multicultural society, for every community has its own culture. To create this stronger society, leaders must look beyond their own particular concerns and help their communities respond to problems affecting the larger society in which we live. This includes responding to dogmatists and triumphalists with a demand for pluralism and dialogue.

The Ultimate Truth

Pluralism is difficult enough to maintain when leaders are coping with differences of history, language, and practice. It is doubly hard to sustain a pluralistic approach when dealing with competing claims of ultimate truth. That is why theological claims are so hard to frame within the context of pluralism. Yet if congregational communities are to have anchoring roles in stabilizing American society, that is precisely what we must do. So how can we maintain pluralism in the face of competing claims of exclusive truth?

The first response is based on the belief that Mom loves me enough. It goes like this: I feel God's love, and, like other human beings, I have been blessed with enough of God's love. I feel certain of that. Therefore I do not need to assert that "God loves me more than God loves you."

The second response grows out of my understanding of multiculturalism and my recognition that the beliefs of those with whom I disagree are as authentic as mine. That response is framed this way: You believe in the divine authority and revelation of the scripture of your community. I believe in the scripture of my community. My roots are in my culture and my community's way of living, and my roots nurture me. I will not uproot myself, and I will not ask you to, either. Neither of us can objectively prove the truth of our own claim or the falsehood of the other's claim. Let us instead accept each other's sincerity and integrity.

The third response springs from an approach found in Jewish tradition. Occasionally, the Rabbis of the Talmud debate until they come to a stand-still, and it becomes clear that neither side can demonstrate that its view is right. The debate is declared a tie to be resolved in messianic days. We need to recognize that religious claims to exclusive truth require us to postpone the final decision. Until messianic days we need to acknowledge and respect the certainty that each of us feels in our own belief.

These three responses are not mutually exclusive. On the contrary, each draws strength from the others. Together they sustain my pluralism. But what if there are moral questions at stake? Then we must do our best to resolve them while also recognizing that my theological claims and definitions will have little influence on you, and yours will have little meaning to me. Recognizing each other's integrity and authenticity, we must struggle to find ways to create a dialogue about the hard issues that allows us to live together in our larger society. That requires patience and the understanding that those who are shaking their fists at us today may come to share our views tomorrow. Theological claims are made, after all, by people of faith!

One example of that process occurred among American Jews. Bat mitzvah ceremonies, the counterpart for girls of bar mitzvah ceremonies for boys, were invented by Mordecai Kaplan and celebrated by Reconstructionist Jews beginning in 1922. Many opposed the change, sometimes expressing themselves in deeply hostile ways. Most Reform Jews opposed it because it strengthened a ceremony they had already ceased performing for boys, and the Conservative and Orthodox opposed it because it signaled more progressive change than they were willing to make at the time. The leaders of the other Jewish movements gradually overcame their resistance to this innovation until today it is practiced not only throughout the Reform and Conservative movements but increasingly among Orthodox Jews as well.

Not all moral conflicts will be resolved by the passage of time, but many will. When I find myself locked in a conflict, I try to step back and gain perspective. We are both certain we are right, and yet at least one of us is wrong. Only with the passage of time—and perhaps not until messianic days—will we know whose view is correct. Together we can search for a path that lets us walk side by side, carrying our conflicting certainties. I believe that true theological leadership exemplifies and teaches that kind of maturity and integrity.

7

COMMUNITY AND SPIRITUALITY

A hermit's life of solitude brings about harmony with natural rhythms and helps cultivate an innner stillness that gives perspective and encourages an awareness of the inner link to transcendence. Living alone encourages you to come to terms with yourself.

Life in community provides a different set of opportunities for transcendence. Glimmers of transcendence shine through in the love that binds us together, in religious ritual, and in acts of moral courage or the willingness of individuals to do the right thing even when it may be dangerous. These are what Peter Berger, the famed sociologist of religion, has called signals of transcendence, or rumors of angels.

A community that seeks justice and gentleness, beauty and caring, is concerned with transcendence and the religious aspect of human life, even if its members have never thought about it that way. A strong community links people together with spiritual bonds and encourages us to find meaning in who we are and what we do. Community building is thus a religious act that itself is a signal of transcendence.

Often we listen so hard for the thunderbolt that we miss the soft whisper of transcendence we really want to hear. That whisper is always present in authentic community; we need only listen with an ear attuned to its soft tones. Authentic community is a holy thing.

ON BEING HOLY

One of my favorite biblical verses is the one from Leviticus that proclaims, "You shall be holy, for I your God am holy." This introduces the Holiness Code, a huge list of ethical and ritual precepts that constitute the Bible's description of what we need to do if we want to be holy.

Acting holy isn't restricted to people who think of themselves as pious. Every moral action, every ritual that confirms the meaning in human life, every attempt to make the life of the community better is a holy act. We can discover that by listening very closely for the whisper of transcendence. When we treat each person as having ultimate worth, as being made in the image of God, we can hear the rumor of angels.

Anyone who has taken part in community life knows about the conflicts, the frustrations, the anger, and the self-seeking that can be found there. Where is the holiness in that? It is in the overcoming and the overlooking, in the letting go of anger and the soothing of the ruffled spirit. Sometimes holiness emerges when we redirect our anger so that it stimulates pangs of conscience or improved conduct.

Communities often require careful negotiation and compromise. They struggle over power issues and decision-making processes. Some people consider these activities profane, if not worse. I don't think so. If we keep our eyes focused on purposes of transcendent worth, mean what we say and say what we mean, and act out of gentleness and a desire not to hurt, then we are doing holy work in a holy way.

The gritty work of building community creates the space for developing the loving side in people. It is certainly as holy as scouring an altar or bringing an offering or reciting a prayer, provided that the person who does it is aware of the need to listen for the whisper of transcendence that can keep us on a holy path. The challenge is to do the meeting, discussing, and negotiating with the consciousness that this too is holy work.

Seeking Unity and Harmony

The Jewish prayer that is used to divide the sections of the service, to mark the end of study, and to conclude worship, a prayer often recited by mourners, is called the kaddish, literally sanctification. Its last line begins, "May the One who makes peace above make peace among us." The word *peace* is *shalom* in Hebrew, a word that encompasses multiple meanings, from completeness to harmony and unity. To add to the completeness, harmony, and unity of the world is a holy aspiration. Bringing *shalom* within a community or between communities is a wondrous thing. This task, too, is a spiritual task. It requires a particular religious orientation.

Parker Palmer, an active Quaker, wrote:

> If my private perceptions are the measure of truth, if my truth cannot be challenged or enlarged by the perceptions of another, I have merely found one more way to objectify and hold the other at arm's length, to avoid again the challenge of personal transformation. This view isolates the self, creates as many worlds as

there are knowers, destroys the possibility of community, and finally makes the other an object of no real account.*

This destructive isolation of the individual from other people is truly unholy. Assuming the actions are moral, all things that create a greater unity or a more harmonious whole among people and between people and their physical world are holy.

This spiritual goal of bringing about harmony, unity, ecological restoration, and transcendence may often be fostered by people who would not describe their motives or actions as holy. But when they are acting for these purposes, holiness infuses what they do and think; it sustains them even if they do not recognize it. Just as a baby would fail to thrive without love, so we would die without caring, hope, and meaning. God is present in the love, caring, and hope that are bound up in our will to live and love. Those who seek community and harmony are seeking to make the Divine manifest in our world.

COMMUNITY AND PHILOSOPHY

I spent several days at Kripalu, a meditation center nestled in the Berkshire Mountains near Lenox, Massachusetts. The daily rhythm of yoga, meditation, and community service creates an atmosphere of calm, internally focused living, which is remarkably restorative. I was struck by the fact that the Hindu religious life of that community could be found

---

*Parker Palmer, *To Know As We Are Known: A Spirituality of Education* (New York: HarperCollins, 1993), p. 54.

everywhere—in the artwork, the choice of Sanskrit names for community initiates, the lit candles on altars during yoga and meditation, the modes of communal expression, the rituals and ceremonies, the community's rules.

Part of what makes Kripalu such a powerfully effective community is how clearly its daily functioning reflects its philosophy. Most of the community members work at the center and therefore spend much of their daily lives in shared space. This intensifies the experience, but it only works because the members promise to follow the philosophy and practice of the community as long as they are there. I could not stay long in that community because I am not a Hindu, but for those who are, it offers extraordinary spiritual riches.

Underlying the power of the Kripalu community is a shared rhythm of daily life in consonance with its philosophy. The spiritual intensity of any community is largely determined by how well the philosophy and action of the community are integrated, and by how its explicitly spiritual practices are incorporated into the daily life of the community. For those who care about spiritual depth and intensity, that is an exciting challenge.

Theology in Hiding

Every community has its own philosophy. Some, like Kripalu's, are explicit and carefully thought out, which results in a strong, focused community.

Sometimes, however, the group's philosophy is only implicit. I recently met with a charitable group whose members insisted that they operate in a completely secular and businesslike way. The moment they began setting priorities, however, they started making value judgments that were far from morally neutral. Sometimes their values were rooted in the Jewish backgrounds of the group's members; sometimes their values stemmed from the group's history or American culture. There was no consensus about which values would be invoked when. These leaders were clearly basing decisions on values, but since these values were implicit rather than explicit, the leaders were unable to examine their value choices and determine whether their underlying philosophy was one they could all support. Because they did not consciously acknowledge their philosophy and values, the group remained unfocused and ineffective. Their failure to clarify their philosophy was handicapping their community.

Every community with a significant history has a guiding philosophy, and hiding within any guiding philosophy is always a little bit of theology. As soon as we talk about the unity of all humanity or mutual commitment for a harmonious community or improving our world, we are implying something about how we think the world ultimately works. Philosophies cannot avoid dealing with theological questions like what life is all about and what that has to do with religious traditions or our relationship with God. Denying that we need to deal with those things is a theological statement in itself. It says that our religious paths need not shape our whole lives.

From the community's philosophy and values—and its underlying theology—comes its shared understanding of how people make the Divine manifest in the world. When a community's guiding principles remain implicit and vague, individuals remain only loosely connected to one another, and the community and its vision suffer. But when a community's philosophy and values are explicitly stated, as at Kripalu, it is openly manifested in ritual, ceremonies, and daily living. As a result, members of the community develop strong interpersonal relationships, and the community gains strength, focus, and momentum.

THE CENTER OF THE COMMUNITY

The mission, vision, and purpose of a community help tie members together. Martin Buber, the theologian whose most important work, *I and Thou,* was published in the 1920s, taught that what binds an authentic community together is its collective understanding of what is ultimately important, and its shared experience, which reinforces that understanding. Like a magnet that pulls a confused pile of iron filings into a beautiful pattern as a result of a shared orientation, a shared vision of ultimacy moves members from an amorphous crowd into the beauty of community. Buber called this orientation a shared connection to God.

Buber was referring to the kind of authentic, intensive community we have been discussing. Other kinds of community have many useful functions, and they are necessary parts of societies structured like ours, but they generally lack this clear sense of purpose, which gives the community its orientation and unity.

A community that shares this sense of ultimacy, purpose, and unity also manifests authentic relationships born from the intimate connections rooted in the community's core values. These relationships embody honesty and caring, and share a moral and spiritual basis in the central vision of the community. Shared beliefs and lifestyles make it possible for every member of a small community to have a relationship with every other member.

Despite best intentions, many kinds of corruption may

creep into community life. Leaders may lose sight of their sacred trust and place personal gain ahead of community welfare. The community itself may dissolve into factionalism, become mired in routine, or fail to adapt to changing conditions, eroding the fabric of community life from within. When that happens, the community does not fully become a community again until it renews its vision and recommits itself to its core values.

Many people reject community living because they see the shell of community structures without an inner connection to what ultimately matters. I would say to them, "Settle for no substitute!" Real communities have a central vision, orientation, and spiritual groundedness. From that center comes transforming power!

COMMUNITY DISCIPLINE

In traditional Jewish life, prayer is mandated three times a day. The laws of kashrut and the blessings surrounding eating shape this most basic of activities and elevate it to a sacramental act. The celebration of Shabbat and the restrictions it imposes—such as not cooking or driving a car—give structure to our weekly rhythm. Rules govern many aspects of daily living. These form a natural discipline for people who adhere to them as part of a Jewish community. Embedded in this shared rhythm and daily practice lies a highly developed spiritual form that has enormous power.

The same is true of life in the Kripalu community, and in Catholic and Buddhist monasteries. Some secular communities have their own ideologies and daily life rhythms. Communes and kibbutzim are often founded based on specific ideologies. Over time, however, it is difficult to maintain the ideologies and disciplines in secular settings because increased affluence and the passage of time tend to overpower these original reasons and make individualism and autonomy seem more important.

Communities thrive to the degree that the disciplines of the community are practiced by everyone. These disciplines bind people together through shared experience. Community grows weaker when people do not follow the same life rhythms and embrace the same opportunities for spiritual contemplation and renewal, eroding the community's capacity to make moral demands. As people go their separate ways, community members have less to lose when they say no.

In a voluntary community, we receive the gift of community connection through shared disciplines and life rhythms. In each of them are spiritual gifts that we discover only when we lovingly accept each repetition and openly seek what each new repetition has to offer.

Freedom and Law

My friend Michael Strassfeld told me about a gathering at Weiss's Farm in New Jersey that brought together members of *havurot,* Jewish fellowship groups, from all over the country. Everyone there (or their parents) had abandoned large chunks of Jewish law as practiced by the Orthodox for moral or practical reasons. The people who gathered at Weiss's Farm, many of them part of the 1960s counterculture, were talking about how to develop a shared communal practice. It was suggested that the group appoint some people to put together a new set of regulations, a new *halakha,* that could then be voted on by the group as a whole. After some debate, Michael asked who would follow the parts of the new *halakha* with which they disagreed. Not a single hand was raised, and the proposal died then and there.

For a discipline to work, it must be embraced by the members of a community, it must reflect the orienting vision of that community, and the community's members must believe that it gives them more than it costs them. Given our contemporary attachment to autonomy, that is a tough order to fill. The people at Weiss's Farm did not have a single shared community. And they would not commit themselves to more than what was needed to keep their community gathering together.

That is the key to developing the shared spiritual disciplines of a community. How much discipline is needed to keep together the kind of community, the kind of shared life, that the members of the community want? That may be the determinant of how much spiritual discipline the community can begin with. But for those involved in a radiant center, disciplines of other sorts may well be added. Additional study and shared living arrangements may also offer opportunities for life rhythms to develop and grow into disciplines. As shared living deepens, so do its rewards. This may engender a willingness to expand shared practice yet more. As this happens, the community grows in intensity and commitment.

If this gradual, measured approach is taken, many varieties of discipline and practice will spring up within the same community. To keep things from becoming chaotic, the community must take extra care to teach its members about its spiritual center. To avoid stagnating at one level of discipline and practice, the leaders must take an active role in teaching, modeling, and encouraging people to move toward greater observance.

In this kind of multilayered community, it is much more difficult to maintain a sense of coherence than it is in a more strictly observant community. The teaching and politics of a pluralistic community require a more sophisticated approach to sustain momentum and avoid frustrating those who are more committed. It is easy to be distracted by people less committed and disciplined; that is why monasteries restrict membership. Yet while maintaining coherence is a challenge, one way to accomplish this is for people to take responsibility for teaching others what they have recently learned. This creates circles of learning pointed toward the center.

In addition, leaders need to find opportunities for nurturing their own spiritual life and renewing its vigor. Leaders cannot effectively usher others onto paths that they themselves do not travel. While more profound leaders may lead shallow communities, shallow leaders cannot create or sustain spiritually rich communities.

When guests visit, they will feel the spiritual and emotional pull of the community even as the lure of autonomy pushes them away. Some will be caught up in the community's rhythms, come to recognize its spiritual center, and move toward becoming members. The meaning of their connection will then gradually open for them like a blooming of the heart.

ROMANTIC OR REAL?

Most places that call themselves communities are not like this. Most of the communities in America have come to accommodate the high value placed on individual autonomy and materialism in American culture. They often invoke the language of community without making a serious commitment to its underlying content. That would require a substantial commitment to intrinsic goods and joint communal living.

We all know that we would like a feeling of connection to others, a sense of comfortable belonging. And we miss that enough to have a romantic and even sentimental wish for its return. With sincerity and goodwill, some institutions encourage acts of covenantal commitment toward those in need. That gives some meaningful content to the rhetoric. But these important steps are but a modest beginning. Romantic longing alone cannot build meaningful community. Communities ultimately need shared vision and practice.

In his *Guide to the Perplexed,* the medieval philosopher Maimonides draws an analogy between seeking the truth and making a long and arduous journey to a palace. When all our romantic and sentimental hopes are placed on the first small steps toward creating community, we are tempted to mistake the curb that marks the beginning of the path for the palace itself. That mistake leaves us feeling disappointed that the rhetoric does not match the reality. Moving past the curb is an important first step, but then it takes both discipline and clarity of vision to walk the long way to the palace. The road has both rewards and distractions. It is easy to turn aside and meander in the palace's beautiful garden and then leave the palace's grounds. Only at the end of the journey, in the beauty of the community of the palace, is the purpose of the journey revealed. Only then are freedom and law merged into one.

8

A Shared Jewish Future

One of the peculiarities of Judaism is that it flows from Jewish peoplehood. Jewish ethnicity and Jewish religion cannot be meaningfully separated because they are both rooted in the historical experience of the Jewish people. This gives Jews the advantage and burden of our own languages, art, literature, music, poetry, dance, food, philosophy, customs, superstitions—all the trappings of one of the world's major civilizations.

But a civilization cannot be handed down in privacy. It cannot be handed down just by reading books. To thrive, culture must be lived. When I want to savor matzah balls, reading recipes is not a meaningful substitute. The setting for many important facets of Jewish civilization—eating, child-rearing, and Shabbat observance, for example—is the family. But the family cannot learn and sustain even these aspects of Jewish living by itself, and much of Judaism cannot be experienced just within the family. The only plausible setting for much of Jewish living is the community.

In community, our religion and ethnicity are united in a daily practice that expresses our values and heritage. As a minority group, we can preserve our distinctive heritage only in the context of a community where we can celebrate who we are and reinforce our values and conduct. The need for belonging is so strong that if we live outside intensive Jewish community in a society like America's, what makes us human will urge us to conform to the larger society. After all, people need to belong, or at least fit in. They need to belong not to an imagined community, but to a real one. For our civilization to continue, Jews must live it together, in community.

How Many Communities Do We Need?

One of my favorite rabbinic tales is about the Jew who stops going to pray with the rest of his community three times a day. A few days go by, and the man's rabbi, worried about him, comes to see him at home.

"We've missed you at prayers," the rabbi says. "Are you well?"

"Oh yes," the Jew replies. "I just thought it would be more efficient to pray at home."

Silently, the rabbi reaches a poker into the fireplace where a warm fire is burning. He extracts a red, glowing coal and moves it to the edge of the hearth. Slowly the coal fades, and the rabbi silently watches until the coal turns black and cold. "We all need the warmth of community," says the rabbi.

"I'll see you at morning prayers tomorrow," says the man, and the rabbi takes his leave.

The Mishnah, the oldest codification of rabbinic law, proclaims, "Do not separate yourself from the community." That injunction reflects the reality that it is impossible to sustain Jewish living for any extended period without community. But the community from which we should not separate ourselves is not the amorphous mass known as the American Jewish community. It is a community linked by its vision and practice, and sustained by friendship, trust, and shared experience.

Enormous differences exist among American Jews regarding values like equality for women, matters of aesthetics, and issues of personal belief and practice. American Jews cannot build just one kind of intensive community. There will need to be many. To be successful, each intensive community must reflect the vision and practice of its leaders and members.

Furthermore, community living has always been the primary mode of acculturation. Given human nature, it cannot be otherwise. Through these communities Jews will learn their culture, absorb its norms, beliefs, values, and ideals, and live its rituals and practices. These communities are vital, but they are too small to be self-sufficient. To obtain the resources they need, they have to join together in streams or movements.

The larger Jewish polity will need the support of those in intensive communities to provide collectively those things that no individual community can effectively provide by itself. The Jewish people's ability to sustain the large institutions it needs depends on the successful acculturation and motivation of Jews. That can only happen on a broad scale in intensive communities. It is through intensive communities, in turn, that Jews can become meaningfully linked to the Jewish people as a whole.

ABOUT SYNAGOGUES

Congregations in North America vary enormously in size, scope of program, aspirations, intensity of Jewish living, ideology, and the kinds of people they attract. The best of them contain several radiant centers, aspire to be communities, and set themselves the task of bringing Jews of all ages closer to Jewish living. Regardless of what we might choose to do if we were designing the North American Jewish community from scratch, the congregations in place are our primary instruments of Jewish acculturation. It would be politically impossible and far too expensive to attempt to recreate Jewish living inside other structures.

Nonetheless, we must recognize that most of the congregations as they are now structured cannot function as communities. They are too large to be intimate, unified communities, and it is unreasonable to expect that their members would agree to a sudden shift in the demands placed upon them. Intensive communities within congregations are therefore urgently needed.

Congregations have been creating *havurot*—mini-communities that meet for some combination of study, prayer, socializing, celebration, and social action—within themselves since 1969, eight years after the Reconstructionist movement invented them as freestanding entities. These *havurot* provide a warm social connection for their members, but they rarely offer the acculturation or intensity of strong Jewish communities. For *havurot* to accomplish that, they would need to make a number of significant changes, including meeting with much greater frequency and becoming serious places of study and prayer. They would need vocal support from the congregation's leaders for intensifying their experience and making more demands on their members. Congregations have not wanted *havurot* to become that intense, lest they shift energy away from the synagogue itself.

A shift toward fuller-functioning *havurot* would require the development of a substantial program to train service leaders not only in the mechanics of prayer, but in spiritual techniques and theological issues so that prayer leaders could help *havurah* members deepen their personal prayer experience in small groups. And it would require the training of a large cadre of volunteer educators who could teach texts and Jewish practices, so that instruction could be personalized as people start to reengage with Jewish living.

Most fundamentally, to achieve these goals a congregation would have to reconceptualize itself as a group of interlocking intensive communities rather than as a single community. This is not at all unprecedented. Mordecai Kaplan envisioned multiple-community synagogues many years ago, and several already exist around North America, though they do not yet have aspirations as high as the ones described here.

If the task of providing the primary community for today's Jews is to be taken seriously, the engagement with community, spirituality, education, shared living, social action, moral issues—all the components of genuine communal life—must be vastly greater than it currently is. That is our challenge. The penalties for failure and the rewards for success are infinitely great.

Autonomy and Jewish Community

In response to the North American commitment to individual autonomy, synagogues have kept relatively silent about key issues in people's lives—money, time commitments, family versus career, sexuality, and so on. Yet people expect a community to provide clear guidance about how to live their lives, or at least help in clarifying their thinking about major decisions they face. These two conflicting realities have undermined Jews' commitment to the synagogue.

If we want to create community, we must be prepared to tackle difficult questions once again. Most American Jews do not want to be constrained by inherited Jewish law because its positions partly rest on values and beliefs with which we disagree. At the same time, we do not wish to follow the dictates of the *New York Times* either, because we want our decisions to reflect Jewish thinking and Jewish values. We want to base our decisions on both inherited Jewish tradition and the values we have added to it, values like equality for women, democracy, and inclusion.

To maintain our loyalty, a community must speak to those issues. Just as important, it must help to make the Jewish sources from which its views derive accessible to its members. The community must help us think for ourselves in a Jewish way. Accomplishing that would allow us to synthesize autonomy and involvement in Jewish community. That means teaching us how to read and use traditional sources, which requires the acquisition of language skills. Judaism is a textual tradition. Only when people feel comfortable with classical and contemporary Jewish texts will they feel fully at home in Jewish civilization. That is in no way to discount the importance of music, literature, and the many other facets of Jewish civilization. But Jewish living cannot be divorced from wrestling with sacred Jewish texts.

People don't want to stay in a community where they feel incompetent. If Jewish living is to be genuine, community members will have to be helped to attain a level of competence that builds confidence. That in turn will engender further loyalty and involvement among the community's members. It will also train a new generation in how to add their voices to the rich chorus of Jewish tradition, blending the new with the old to expand on the rich multivocality of Jewish tradition.

RETHINKING JEWISH EDUCATION

In hundreds of meetings in recent years I have participated in endless discussions about how to make Jewish education work. The assumption of these meetings is that if education were done right, it would eliminate the problems associated with the massive assimilation to be found among the Jews of North America, especially intermarriage. If the field of Jewish education were to undertake this by itself, a serious attempt would take many times the amount of money that could possibly be raised for day-school buildings, teacher training, and professional salaries. But even then it would fail, for Jewish education is a support for Jewish living, not a substitute for Jewish living.

In the past, it was assumed that students experienced Jewish living at home and in the synagogue, and that the task of education was to teach skills and meanings that would bolster that experience. That assumption resulted in a misdirected mission. Generations of students who made little sense of religious school will attest to that.

Then came an attempt to provide Jewish experiences as the primary component of Jewish education on the assumption that these experiences had to precede lessons about its significance. This was a correct assumption, but aside from short-term measures like retreats and camps, schools could not provide sufficient primary experience. And when schools tried to do so, the experience was rarely consonant with the rest of the students' lives. Because of the gap, the students usually left that experience behind them when they went home.

The current interest in Jewish family education grew out of the failure of those earlier educational initiatives. The goal here is to help the family assume its rightful place as the center for Jewish living. This is an important step forward because it takes seriously the need to create a context for ongoing Jewish living. But the individual nuclear family is a tiny one-celled creature, alone in the huge American cultural sea. It cannot perform the primary acculturation role by itself, or even in conjunction with the school.

The family needs a significant community context. If Jewish education is going to work, it will have to do so as an adjunct to intensive Jewish community. A vastly increased emphasis on adult Jewish education that imparts skills, concepts, and motivation for spiritual and communal engagement will be a vital part of that. Restructuring of schools, educational missions, and educational curricula, so that they support intensive community and help to create it, is a challenge that cries out for our best educators' attention.

JEWISH COMMUNAL LEADERSHIP

Many hardworking leaders have dedicated much of their adult lives to helping world Jewry and maintaining Jewish communal institutions. Through the admirable efforts of these leaders, these institutions have accomplished many important things. In the tragedies and triumphs of recent Jewish history, they have played vital roles in enabling Jewish survival. But these institutions are for the benefit of Jewry. They are not American Jewry itself.

Jewish communal leaders, like all leaders, lead by example. If Jewish civilization is to thrive, it will have to do so in communities. Culture never exists anywhere else for long. Yet most American Jewish leaders, like most of American Jewry, live outside intensive Jewish community, even though they devote prodigious amounts of time and energy to the work of the Jewish polity's institutions.

That is why the intermarriage rate among the children of communal leaders isn't substantially different from that of most synagogue members. Our leaders have shown extraordinary dedication to the Jewish polity, but by and large they have not embraced intensive personal Jewish living or membership in intensive Jewish communities. American Jewry's leaders have invested their time and energy in cultivating important institutions that do not have the capacity to act as the primary vehicles for sustaining Jewish life.

This is no indictment. These are wonderful, intelligent, dedicated leaders who have dealt with the emergencies of the hour, and nobody told them that would not be enough. However, we now have reached a crossroads. The future of the American Jewish community depends on creating intensive Jewish community. And the leaders we need are those who will take us where we need to go, leading by example and teaching by self-transformation.

We must turn to our leaders and ask them to exemplify the personal study, spiritual growth, and commitment to living in community that is the need of this hour. That is an enormous request because it means rethinking fundamental life patterns. But that is the request we need to make now. We need leaders who model Jewish living, Jewish decision making, and putting intensive Jewish community first. We need professionals and volunteers, men and women, young and old, rabbis, cantors, and educators alongside scholars and social workers.

To this challenge we can apply Herzl's maxim, *"Im tirtsu, eyn zo aggada,"* "If we will it, it need not be just a dream."

THE POSTMODERN JEWISH WORLD

The Jewish experiment with modern autonomy has succeeded beyond our wildest expectations in creating material success. And yet it has brought about an enormous crisis. Community is so fundamental to Judaism that all efforts to replace it have been disastrous.

In the postmodern world, we are now recognizing what we need to do to ease that crisis. Growing numbers of people understand that more material goods will not cure what ails most of us middle-class Americans. They realize, too, that in this age of multiculturalism American culture will not become uniform, regardless of what we might like to see. This opens the way for a reinvigorated American Jewish community to an extent that we could not have predicted even a few years ago. I am positing the need for those committed to American Jewish survival to become members of intensive communities that reflect their values and beliefs.

If American Jews were surveyed today, most of them would certainly say that such a thing is not possible for them. That is usually the reaction when people are asked to make a major change and they haven't yet seen others succeeding at it. The fact that creating intensive community is currently so far from people's thoughts merely tells us how urgent it is that we begin the task of redesigning Jewish communal models, financially backing the training efforts necessary to make them a reality, and publicizing the successes and failures in the enterprise of community building.

The Jewish people has demonstrated over and over again an uncanny ability to recreate itself as changing conditions have demanded. The time has come to do so again. In a world that is changing faster and faster, we can afford to waste no time in bringing the old and new together in the form of the Jewish community we need for ourselves, our families and friends, and our future.

REDISCOVERING THE CYCLES OF MEANING

Having lived in Philadelphia only six months when my daughter Nomi was born, I didn't really think about how many people might come to her naming, which took place at home a few days after her birth. Imagine my surprise when 120 people showed up. The intensity and excitement of 120 people singing, clapping, and celebrating made it a day never to be forgotten.

Where had all these people come from, and how did they know what to do? They are my family's community. A celebration for any of us is a celebration for all of us. We celebrate Shabbat together, eat, pray, and study together in a way that makes the weekly cycle a community cycle. We celebrate each holiday of the yearly cycle together. And we support each other in the tough moments and celebrate the joys of the life cycle together.

This means much more than personal connections and knowledge of the same tunes. Living together in community brings a shared weekly and yearly rhythm, and shared values. It brings the intimacy of a shared life—greater depth to our joy, greater mutual support for our shared way of living. The meaning of community resonates in our life together.

This kind of community can be built anywhere people want it enough. It can start with one person persuading friends and develop into a formal structure. The only element that must be present to get started is a committed individual. It's not too soon to seek partners for this journey toward greater spiritual meaning.

Appendix I

STRATEGIES FOR ORGANIZING CARING COMMUNITIES

To create a caring community, you begin by finding out what people think needs to be done. That usually requires a committee. It is important to recognize that the people who enjoy meetings and are good at planning are rarely the same people who derive the most satisfaction from carrying out those plans. In the ,first stage, a committee of planners must compile a list of tasks that need doing. This is best done in close consultation with community professionals.

One way to generate the list is to go through the life cycle—pregnancy, birth, religious training, bar and bat mitzvah/confirmation, wedding, divorce, illness, unemployment, death, single adults, and so on. In each case, the group needs to discuss what people's needs are and which ones the community can help meet. In the case of illness, single people dealing with a disease may need to have food brought to their homes, while a young mother who is sick may benefit most from help with carpooling and babysitting. Prolonged illness requires complex, carefully planned support; a different kind of help may be needed in emergencies.

It is important to select high-visibility, simple tasks at the beginning so that community members can experience some "quick wins"—actions that have a major short-term impact on the community without a huge amount of effort. At the beginning, tasks should be kept simple. Someone who might feel very uncomfortable calling up a sick person to ask for a grocery list might instead enjoy purchasing and delivering the items on that list. Someone might be happy to cook a hot meal if told exactly what all the members of a family in need would like.

The committee needs to design tasks that people with different skills and interests are comfortable completing. The person who goes to meet with a family to find out what they need will not necessarily have the skills required to do the family's carpooling or car repair. And vice versa. Most people feel awkward doing tasks that are unclear or open-ended. It is usually easiest to find someone to do a highly specific task. "They need babysitting from 7 to 10 p.m. on Wednesday so that he can visit her at the hospital. The kids will have eaten but might need help with their homework." It's a lot easier to find a cook if that person doesn't have to plan the menu. Arrangements about who pays for groceries and other expenses should be explicit from the beginning, so both recipients and volunteers know where they stand.

Members of the organizing committee might each be in charge of one kind of life-cycle need. The person in charge should work out a detailed list of what help can be made available, so that when a meeting is arranged with those in need, offers of specific help can be made. This saves time and makes it easier to assign tasks to volunteers. As the number of people who benefit from deeds of caring grows and as the number of people who find satisfaction in help-ing and/or developing friendships through the network of caring grows, the community can take on larger numbers of tasks as well as tasks of greater duration and complexity.

It is helpful to recruit volunteers in advance. Once a year, members of Kehillath Israel in Pacific Palisades, California, hand out a card with different tasks listed around all the edges and ask congregants to turn down the tabs of each activity they are willing to help with. Lists of potential volunteers are then compiled, and each list is turned over to the person in charge of that activity. In this way people can volunteer where they feel most comfortable. Once they get their feet wet, they can gradually be encouraged to take on more complex tasks that require more commitment.

Some people will be happier helping with rituals, such as joining in a minyan at the home of a mourner. Others will prefer cooking, running errands, spending time with children, or visiting the sick. The larger the array of choices, the more likely it is that more people will participate. For the sake of community building, it is important to involve as many people as possible; that means committee members should take on few tasks themselves, opening the way for others to participate.

One key to success is publicizing these efforts. People feel good when they know their community is helping others. And they need to know what is going on if they are to volunteer or to ask for help. Information about how to ask for help in a confidential way should be distributed regularly. Volunteers should be publicly recognized and thanked. The importance of the project should be addressed in sermons and written about in bulletins. To that end, first-person accounts from both volunteers and beneficiaries can be both moving and motivating.

Communities can help in sometimes surprising ways. A corporate accountant in my community helps families in financial trouble create a new budget and refinance their debts when this sort of highly confidential help is suggested by the rabbi of the congregation. A social worker helps people with referrals for counseling and social services. It probably would never have occurred to the accountant or the social worker to volunteer to do these things, but they are happy to do them now that they have been asked. Several businesspeople in one community joined together at the suggestion of their rabbi to create an interest-free loan fund to help people get through financial emergencies. The possibilities are endless. As the activity level grows, the organizing committee will need to develop strong subcommittees in order to effectively tap the talents of the volunteers. Eventually this network will touch everyone in the community— some as volunteers, some as beneficiaries, and, eventually, most people as both.

Aiding the poor, building interfaith dialogue, campaigning for legal change, and teaching reading are but a few of the myriad forms of improving our world through education, exercising compassion, and pursuing justice. Many congregations have a single committee devoted to this whole range of activity. In these cases, only a small number of people are involved in organizing the activity, and that limits how much can get done. Different kinds of people find different projects meaningful. Some prefer one-day commitments, while others want to do something each week. Some prefer organizing tasks, while others prefer to develop long-term relationships with people they are helping. Some like to use their professional skills; others want to do something completely different. Because there are so many ways to improve our world and there is so much work to be done, it is important to provide a variety of opportunities so that everyone in the community can derive satisfaction from giving of themselves. Only then will it be easy to create an expectation that everyone will take part, including those motivated to perform direct service and those motivated to effect political change, those who prefer organizing and those who enjoy physical labor or direct contact.

Ideally there should be a central steering committee that helps to recruit volunteers, publicize projects, and coordinate efforts. Then each project will have its own subcommittee or task force. At first, the professionals and the steering committee may need to brainstorm to come up with possible task forces and recruit leaders for them. As the community becomes accustomed to these ongoing volunteer efforts, community members may well start to come forward with projects that they wish to undertake.

Regular publicity about task force successes, moving experiences, and names of participants will bolster volunteer recruitment efforts. Sermons, bulletin articles, and stories in the city's newspapers will all reinforce participants' awareness of the importance of what they are doing and boost their motivation and sense of accomplishment. Personally recruiting each community member for task forces each year will result in a vastly higher rate of participation, as will offering a variety of choices in terms of issues, duration, and the nature of involvement.

Social action can often be an intergenerational undertaking—teenagers work wonderfully with adults on projects like Habitat for Humanity, which has extraordinary side benefits in terms of relationship building. One youth group I know of delivers food baskets to the ill and the elderly the day before every major religious holiday.

A critical part of volunteer education involves teaching about the underlying values expressed in religious texts that motivate work on a particular project. Sometimes discussing even a single sentence can make a difference. Starting each session with study or prayer can help to connect the activity to the community's moral and spiritual vision. This inspires both commitment to the project and deeper attachment to the community's values.

Controversial political issues such as abortion rights, school vouchers, or peace in the Middle East have the potential for dividing the community, so it is important to decide how to handle them before they become sources of friction. One simple way to do this is to allow any task force to form that has a sufficient number of members interested in the same approach. Each task force may then be restricted to speaking only in its own name (e.g., the Middle East Task Force of Congregation Shalom), if anyone on the social action committee objects to the full community name being used. This of course creates the possibility that two task forces with conflicting perspectives will form on some issues, but that may also lead to important community programming and discussion, and may motivate people who tend not to express their views to become engaged with issues they truly care about.

It is sometimes easiest and most effective to organize a new activity in the community by joining forces with an already existing organization such as a local food bank, literacy program, lobbying group, or neighborhood interfaith council. At other times it is best to organize an activity from scratch. Careful planning before a project begins will conserve volunteer resources, increase the likelihood of success, and usually leave people more willing to do similar projects in the future. Organizers should discuss their plans with people involved in similar projects so they can tap into existing resources without duplicating effort and avoid common pitfalls that might waste time or money. The staff members of denominational bodies and political organizations can usually recommend experts with whom to consult.

Some people prefer to keep all controversy out of community projects. But if part of the community's purpose is to improve the moral life of its members and the society in which they live, avoiding this kind of issue will prevent the community from fulfilling its own aims. Educating both community members and the public about critical issues is itself an important social action activity. In most communities it is the noncontroversial activities—the walk to raise money for breast cancer prevention or the effort to collect, refurbish, and distribute toys for needy children—that attract the largest number of people and the greatest amount of ongoing energy. But both direct service and engagement with difficult political issues figure prominently in most faith communities. Learning how to handle controversy so that it serves a higher purpose is a critical part of creating a morally vigorous community. People naturally look to their community for help in dealing with difficult issues. A successful community in an open society responds to that need while pursuing the welfare of society at large.

Appendix II

INTERFAITH DIALOGUE, RELIGIOUS VALUES, AND PUBLIC POLICY

Values taught by religious groups have shaped public decisions throughout the history of the United States. "Life, liberty, and the pursuit of happiness" have been defined as inalienable human rights since the establishment of our republic. This view of human rights is grounded in claims about the origins and purpose of our species that go beyond science into matters of belief and theology. Demands for justice and compassion grow out of shared values taught by religious institutions. For the most part, religious groups in America share these fundamental views. The outcry for preserving compassion and justice in America would lose much of its power were it not for the support of local and national religious bodies. Interfaith cooperation on these issues has enhanced religious influence in American life. When this occurs, most people praise the role of religion in public life.

When the denominations are divided, however, charges are made that groups are improperly imposing their will on public life. But our religious beliefs undergird our values and actions, so suggesting that we leave our values out of our public policy thinking makes no sense. In the United States, which guarantees freedom of speech, we should not prevent clergy from speaking their minds on the issues of the day, nor should the official positions of religious bodies have no influence. I passionately disagree, for example, with the Catholic stance on abortion, but I would not want to live in a society where Catholics were blocked from attempting to influence public opinion and political positions on abortion.

Rather than decreasing the involvement of religious groups in the public arena, we need to increase the voice of religion in public life by encouraging the public teaching of values and faith-based definitions. Like Catholics, Jews believe life to be sacred. Unlike them, Jews believe a fetus is not a living person until it can be viable outside the womb. The abortion debate fundamentally hinges on whose definition will be the basis for law.

We can address issues in a more profound and comprehensive way if we each state our premises openly as part of public discourse, acknowledge the origins of our positions, and make the most cogent cases for them that we can. That can be done without resorting to any form of coercion and without in any way privileging religious language or institutions in public forums. Those with more fundamentalist views feel most comfortable using religious rhetoric in the public domain; for the sake of creating the fullest possible discussion of issues, religious liberals need to do likewise. Such an undertaking would place values front and center as critical shapers of public discourse. These values have a power far beyond their religious origins and the issues they are invoked to address. Making them part of public discourse can stimulate participants in that discourse to internalize those values.

That process will create a more morally vigorous citizenry without risking the establishment of religion, as it reveals the moral and religious underpinnings of secular positions. The dispute over allowing same-sex couples to marry is one example. Fundamentalist biblical interpretation—which supports patriarchy and oppression of gay people—should be openly countered by the liberal religious position, which emphasizes the egalitarianism and inclusion implied by *tselem elohim*—that human beings are all created in the image of God.

Encouraging values-based religious discourse in all its diversity will help reinvigorate American moral life by helping us bring to light the religious and moral roots of our public policy. The more substantive discourse that results can actually help steer us away from enfranchising religious symbols and rituals in the public domain yet, at the same time, help us deepen our moral commitments.

SUGGESTIONS FOR FURTHER READING

ABOUT JEWISH CONGREGATIONAL LIFE

Dr. Isa Aron has written two books about congregational transformation, particularly as it pertains to Jewish learning:

> *The Self-Renewing Congregation: Organizational Strategies for Revitalizing Congregational Life.* Woodstock, VT: Jewish Lights, 2002.

> *Becoming a Congregation of Learners: Learning as a Key to Revitalizing Congregational Life.* Woodstock, VT: Jewish Lights, 2000.

The Jewish Reconstructionist Federation has published several workbooks filled with sample congregational materials that can serve as models for congregations undergoing change:

> *Kehillah Builders: Jewish Values-Based Approaches to Building Sacred Reconstructionist Community.* Wyncote, PA: Reconstructionist Press, 2002.

> *A Sacred Trust: A Values-Based Approach to Jewish Communal Leadership and Congregational Governance.* Wyncote, PA: Reconstructionist Press, 2001.

A Torah of Money: Values and Your Community. Wyncote, PA: Reconstructionist Press, 1999.

Schwarz profiles four cutting-edge congregations, one from each denomination in American Jewish life, and uses their characteristics to propose a new paradigm for the American synagogue.

Finding a Spiritual Home: How a Generation of Jews Can Transform the American Synagogue. Woodstock, VT: Jewish Lights, 2003.

In this book, Shawn Zevit explores a number of issues related to congregation-building, with an emphasis on concrete steps for taking a values-based approach to congregational life:

Offerings of the Heart: Jewish Values and Money in Faith Communities. Bethesda, MD: Alban Institute, 2005.

ABOUT CONGREGATION STUDIES

While many of the publications in this field reflect the Christian orientation of their writers, frequently they are easily adapted for Jewish use.

Gary Gunderson, a Christian activist, offers insights into congregational life:

Deeply Woven Roots: Improving the Quality of Life in Your Congregation. Minneapolis: Fortress Press, 1997.

For suggestions on how to create and maintain covenantal commitment within congregations, Gilbert Rendle's book is a treasure trove:

> *Behavioral Covenants in Congregations: A Handbook for Honoring Differences.* Bethesda, MD: Alban Institute, 1999.

Gilbert Rendle has also produced an excellent manual for processes that create dynamism and success in congregational life, particularly for those who anticipate challenges during the period of change:

> *Leading Change in the Congregation: Spiritual and Organizational Tools for Leaders.* Bethesda, MD: Alban Institute, 1998.

For guidance about creating and managing congregational change—and particularly for the group dynamics involved—Peter L. Steinke's volume is a wonderful resource:

> *Healthy Congregations: A Systems Approach.* Bethesda, MD: Alban Institute, 1996.

ABOUT SPIRITUALITY AND RITUAL

Stuart M. Matlins, publisher of Jewish Lights, has edited an anthology of fifty short essays, each dealing with different aspects of Jewish spirituality. Taken together, they offer a host of insights to those walking the path of spiritual discovery:

> *The Jewish Lights Spirituality Handbook: A Guide to Understanding, Exploring and Living a Spiritual Life.* Woodstock, VT: Jewish Lights, 2001.

Debra Orenstein outlines ways the Jewish community can change its liturgy and rituals in response to the evolving nature of contemporary life:

Lifecycles, Vol. 1: Jewish Women on Life Passages and Personal Milestones. Woodstock, VT: Jewish Lights, 1994.

Judea and Ruth Pearl have edited a collection of essays written by almost 150 Jews—both famous and ordinary, from all walks of life, from all around the world—about Judaism and why it matters to them. These essays provide considerable motivation for renewing Jewish commitment:

> *I Am Jewish: Personal Reflections Inspired by the Last Words of Daniel Pearl.* Woodstock, VT: Jewish Lights, 2005.

Michael Strassfeld's book is a moving and penetrating exploration of the joys, insights, and disciplines of spiritually serious Jewish living:

> *A Book of Life: Embracing Judaism as a Spiritual Practice.* New York: Schocken Books, 2002.

This website is rich in resources for revitalizing ritual, adding fresh approaches to prayer, and shaping life-cycle events:

> www.ritualwell.org.

The philosophical issues that underlie this book are explored in the books listed in the bibliography that follows. The works by Bellah and Stout are good places to start.

Bibliography

Ackoff, Russell. *Creating the Corporate Future.* New York: John Wiley, 1981.

Bellah, Robert, Richard Madsen, William Sullivan, Ann Swidler, Steven Tipton. *Habits of the Heart.* San Francisco: Harper and Row, 1986.

———. *The Good Society.* New York: Knopf, 1991.

Berger, Peter, and Thomas Luckmann. *The Social Construction of Reality.* Garden City, NY: Anchor, 1966.

Buber, Martin. *I and Thou.* New York: Scribners, 1970.

Etzioni, Amitai. *The Spirit of Community.* New York: Crown Publishers, 1973.

———. *The Moral Dimension.* New York: Free Press, 1990.

Geertz, Clifford. *The Interpretation of Culture.* New York: Basic Books, 1973.

Hoffman, Lawrence. *The Art of Public Prayer: Not for Clergy Only.* Woodstock, VT: SkyLight Paths, 1999.

MacIntyre, Alasdair. *After Virtue.* South Bend, IN: University of Notre Dame Press, 1984.

Putnam, Robert. *Making Democracy Work: Civic Traditions in*

Modern Italy. Princeton, NJ: Princeton University Press, 1993.

Schein, Edgar. *Organizational Culture and Leadership*. San Francisco: Jossey-Bass, 1985.

Stout, Jeffrey. *Ethics after Babel*. Boston: Beacon Press, 1988.

Taylor, Charles. *The Ethics of Authenticity*. Cambridge, MA: Harvard University Press, 1985.

Williams, Bernard. *Ethics and the Limits of Philosophy*. Cambridge, MA: Harvard University Press, 1985.

Wuthnow, Robert. *Sharing the Journey*. New York: Free Press, 1994.

Notes

Notes

About Jewish Lights

People of all faiths and backgrounds yearn for books that attract, engage, educate, and spiritually inspire.

Our principal goal is to stimulate thought and help all people learn about who the Jewish People are, where they come from, and what the future can be made to hold. While people of our diverse Jewish heritage are the primary audience, our books speak to people in the Christian world as well and will broaden their understanding of Judaism and the roots of their own faith.

We bring to you authors who are at the forefront of spiritual thought and experience. While each has something different to say, they all say it in a voice that you can hear.

Our books are designed to welcome you and then to engage, stimulate, and inspire. We judge our success not only by whether or not our books are beautiful and commercially successful, but by whether or not they make a difference in your life.

For your information and convenience, at the back of this book we have provided a list of other Jewish Lights books you might find interesting and useful. They cover all the categories of your life:

Bar/Bat Mitzvah
Bible Study / Midrash
Children's Books
Congregation Resources
Current Events / History
Ecology
Fiction: Mystery, Science Fiction
Grief / Healing
Holidays / Holy Days
Inspiration
Kabbalah / Mysticism / Enneagram

Life Cycle
Meditation
Parenting
Prayer
Ritual / Sacred Practice
Spirituality
Theology / Philosophy
Travel
Twelve Steps
Women's Interest

Stuart M. Matlins, Publisher

Or phone, fax, mail or e-mail to: **JEWISH LIGHTS** Publishing
Sunset Farm Offices, Route 4 • P.O. Box 237 • Woodstock, Vermont 05091
Tel: (802) 457-4000 • Fax: (802) 457-4004 • www.jewishlights.com
Credit card orders: (800) 962-4544 (8:30AM–5:30PM ET Monday–Friday)
Generous discounts on quantity orders. SATISFACTION GUARANTEED. Prices subject to change.

For more information about each book, visit our website at www.jewishlights.com

Children's Books

What You Will See Inside a Synagogue
By Rabbi Lawrence A. Hoffman and Dr. Ron Wolfson; Full-color photos by Bill Aron

A colorful, fun-to-read introduction that explains the ways and whys of Jewish worship and religious life. Full-page photos; concise but informative descriptions of the objects used, the clergy and laypeople who have specific roles, and much more. For ages 6 & up.

8½ x 10½, 32 pp, Full-color photos, Hardcover, ISBN 1-59473-012-1 **$17.99** *(A SkyLight Paths book)*

Because Nothing Looks Like God
By Lawrence and Karen Kushner

What is God like? Introduces children to the possibilities of spiritual life. Real-life examples of happiness and sadness invite us to explore, together with our children, the questions we all have about God.

11 x 8½, 32 pp, Full-color illus., ISBN 1-58023-092-X **$16.95** *For ages 4 & up*

Also Available: **Because Nothing Looks Like God Teacher's Guide**
8½ x 11, 22 pp, PB, ISBN 1-58023-140-3 **$6.95** *For ages 5–8*

Board Book Companions to *Because Nothing Looks Like God*
5 x 5, 24 pp, Full-color illus., SkyLight Paths Board Books *For ages 0–4*

What Does God Look Like? ISBN 1-893361-23-3 **$7.95**

How Does God Make Things Happen? ISBN 1-893361-24-1 **$7.95**

Where Is God? ISBN 1-893361-17-9 **$7.99**

The 11th Commandment: Wisdom from Our Children
by The Children of America

"If there were an Eleventh Commandment, what would it be?" Children of many religious denominations across America answer in their own drawings and words.
8 x 10, 48 pp, Full-color illus., Hardcover, ISBN 1-879045-46-X **$16.95** *For all ages*

Jerusalem of Gold: Jewish Stories of the Enchanted City
Retold by Howard Schwartz. Full-color illus. by Neil Waldman.

A beautiful and engaging collection of historical and legendary stories for children. Based on Talmud, midrash, Jewish folklore, and mystical and Hasidic sources.
8 x 10, 64 pp, Full-color illus., Hardcover, ISBN 1-58023-149-7 **$18.95** *For ages 7 & up*

The Book of Miracles: A Young Person's Guide to Jewish Spiritual Awareness
By Lawrence Kushner. All-new illustrations by the author.
6 x 9, 96 pp, 2-color illus., Hardcover, ISBN 1-879045-78-8 **$16.95** *For ages 9–13*

In Our Image: God's First Creatures
By Nancy Sohn Swartz
9 x 12, 32 pp, Full-color illus., Hardcover, ISBN 1-879045-99-0 **$16.95** *For ages 4 & up*

Also Available as a Board Book: **How Did the Animals Help God?**
5 x 5, 24 pp, Board, Full-color illus., ISBN 1-59473-044-X **$7.99** *For ages 0–4 (A SkyLight Paths book)*

From SKYLIGHT PATHS PUBLISHING

Becoming Me: A Story of Creation
By Martin Boroson. Full-color illus. by Christopher Gilvan-Cartwright.

Told in the personal "voice" of the Creator, a story about creation and relationship that is about each one of us.
8 x 10, 32 pp, Full-color illus., Hardcover, ISBN 1-893361-11-X **$16.95** *For ages 4 & up*

Ten Amazing People: And How They Changed the World
By Maura D. Shaw. Foreword by Dr. Robert Coles. Full-color illus. by Stephen Marchesi.

Black Elk • Dorothy Day • Malcolm X • Mahatma Gandhi • Martin Luther King, Jr. • Mother Teresa • Janusz Korczak • Desmond Tutu • Thich Nhat Hanh • Albert Schweitzer.

8½ x 11, 48 pp, Full-color illus., Hardcover, ISBN 1-893361-47-0 **$17.95** *For ages 7 & up*

Where Does God Live? *By August Gold and Matthew J. Perlman*

Helps young readers develop a personal understanding of God.
10 x 8½, 32 pp, Full-color photo illus., Quality PB, ISBN 1-893361-39-X **$8.99** *For ages 3–6*

Children's Books
by Sandy Eisenberg Sasso

Adam & Eve's First Sunset: God's New Day
Engaging new story explores fear and hope, faith and gratitude in ways that will delight kids and adults—inspiring us to bless each of God's days and nights.
9 x 12, 32 pp, Full-color illus., Hardcover, ISBN 1-58023-177-2 **$17.95** *For ages 4 & up*

But God Remembered
Stories of Women from Creation to the Promised Land
Four different stories of women—Lillith, Serach, Bityah, and the Daughters of Z—teach us important values through their faith and actions.
9 x 12, 32 pp, Full-color illus., Hardcover, ISBN 1-879045-43-5 **$16.95** *For ages 8 & up*

Cain & Abel: Finding the Fruits of Peace
Shows children that we have the power to deal with anger in positive ways. Provides questions for kids and adults to explore together.
9 x 12, 32 pp, Full-color illus., Hardcover, ISBN 1-58023-123-3 **$16.95** *For ages 5 & up*

God in Between
If you wanted to find God, where would you look? This magical, mythical tale teaches that God can be found where we are: within all of us and the relationships between us.
9 x 12, 32 pp, Full-color illus., Hardcover, ISBN 1-879045-86-9 **$16.95** *For ages 4 & up*

God's Paintbrush: Special 10th Anniversary Edition
Wonderfully interactive, invites children of all faiths and backgrounds to encounter God through moments in their own lives. Provides questions adult and child can explore together.
11 x 8½, 32 pp, Full-color illus., Hardcover, ISBN 1-58023-195-0 **$17.95** *For ages 4 & up*

Also Available: **God's Paintbrush Teacher's Guide**
8½ x 11, 32 pp, PB, ISBN 1-879045-57-5 **$8.95**

God's Paintbrush Celebration Kit
A Spiritual Activity Kit for Teachers and Students of All Faiths, All Backgrounds
Additional activity sheets available:
8-Student Activity Sheet Pack (40 sheets/5 sessions), ISBN 1-58023-058-X **$19.95**
Single-Student Activity Sheet Pack (5 sessions), ISBN 1-58023-059-8 **$3.95**

In God's Name
Like an ancient myth in its poetic text and vibrant illustrations, this award-winning modern fable about the search for God's name celebrates the diversity and, at the same time, the unity of all people.
9 x 12, 32 pp, Full-color illus., Hardcover, ISBN 1-879045-26-5 **$16.99** *For ages 4 & up*

Also Available as a Board Book: **What Is God's Name?**
5 x 5, 24 pp, Board, Full-color illus., ISBN 1-893361-10-1 **$7.99** *For ages 0–4 (A SkyLight Paths book)*

Also Available: **In God's Name video and study guide**
Computer animation, original music, and children's voices. 18 min. **$29.99**

Also Available in Spanish: **El nombre de Dios**
9 x 12, 32 pp, Full-color illus., Hardcover, ISBN 1-893361-63-2 **$16.95** *(A SkyLight Paths book)*

Noah's Wife: The Story of Naamah
When God tells Noah to bring the animals of the world onto the ark, God also calls on Naamah, Noah's wife, to save each plant on Earth. Based on an ancient text.
9 x 12, 32 pp, Full-color illus., Hardcover, ISBN 1-58023-134-9 **$16.95** *For ages 4 & up*

Also Available as a Board Book: **Naamah, Noah's Wife**
5 x 5, 24 pp, Full-color illus., Board, ISBN 1-893361-56-X **$7.95** *For ages 0–4 (A SkyLight Paths book)*

For Heaven's Sake: Finding God in Unexpected Places
9 x 12, 32 pp, Full-color illus., Hardcover, ISBN 1-58023-054-7 **$16.95** *For ages 4 & up*

God Said Amen: Finding the Answers to Our Prayers
9 x 12, 32 pp, Full-color illus., Hardcover, ISBN 1-58023-080-6 **$16.95** *For ages 4 & up*

Current Events/History

The Story of the Jews: A 4,000-Year Adventure—A Graphic History Book
Written & illustrated by Stan Mack
Witty, illustrated narrative of all the major happenings from biblical times to the twenty-first century. 6 x 9, 288 pp., illus., Quality PB, ISBN 1-58023-155-1 **$16.95**

Hannah Senesh: Her Life and Diary, the First Complete Edition
By Hannah Senesh; Foreword by Marge Piercy; Preface by Eitan Senesh
6 x 9, 352 pp, Hardcover, ISBN 1-58023-212-4 **$24.99**

The Jewish Prophet: Visionary Words from Moses and Miriam to Henrietta Szold and A. J. Heschel *By Rabbi Michael J. Shire*
6½ x 8½, 128 pp, 123 full-color illus., Hardcover, ISBN 1-58023-168-3 **Special gift price $14.95**

Shared Dreams: Martin Luther King, Jr. & the Jewish Community
By Rabbi Marc Schneier. Preface by Martin Luther King III.
6 x 9, 240 pp, Hardcover, ISBN 1-58023-062-8 **$24.95**

"Who Is a Jew?": Conversations, Not Conclusions *By Meryl Hyman*
6 x 9, 272 pp, Quality PB, ISBN 1-58023-052-0 **$16.95**

Ecology

Ecology & the Jewish Spirit: Where Nature & the Sacred Meet
Edited by Ellen Bernstein 6 x 9, 288 pp, Quality PB, ISBN 1-58023-082-2 **$16.95**

Torah of the Earth: Exploring 4,000 Years of Ecology in Jewish Thought
Vol. 1: Biblical Israel: One Land, One People; Rabbinic Judaism: One People, Many Lands
Vol. 2: Zionism: One Land, Two Peoples; Eco-Judaism: One Earth, Many Peoples
Edited by Rabbi Arthur Waskow
Vol. 1: 6 x 9, 272 pp, Quality PB, ISBN 1-58023-086-5 **$19.95**
Vol. 2: 6 x 9, 336 pp, Quality PB, ISBN 1-58023-087-3 **$19.95**

Grief/Healing

Against the Dying of the Light: A Parent's Story of Love, Loss and Hope
By Leonard Fein
Unusual exploration of heartbreak and healing. Chronicles the sudden death of author's 30-year-old daughter and shares the wisdom that emerges in the face of loss and grief.
5½ x 8½, 176 pp, Quality PB, ISBN 1-58023-197-7 **$15.99;** Hardcover, ISBN 1-58023-110-1 **$19.95**

Grief in Our Seasons: A Mourner's Kaddish Companion *By Rabbi Kerry M. Olitzky*
4½ x 6½, 448 pp, Quality PB, ISBN 1-879045-55-9 **$15.95**

Healing of Soul, Healing of Body: Spiritual Leaders Unfold the Strength & Solace in Psalms *Edited by Rabbi Simkha Y. Weintraub, C.S.W.*
6 x 9, 128 pp, 2-color illus. text, Quality PB, ISBN 1-879045-31-1 **$14.99**

Jewish Paths toward Healing and Wholeness: A Personal Guide to Dealing with Suffering *By Rabbi Kerry M. Olitzky. Foreword by Debbie Friedman.*
6 x 9, 192 pp, Quality PB, ISBN 1-58023-068-7 **$15.95**

Mourning & Mitzvah, 2nd Edition: A Guided Journal for Walking the Mourner's Path through Grief to Healing *By Anne Brener, L.C.S.W.*
7½ x 9, 304 pp, Quality PB, ISBN 1-58023-113-6 **$19.95**

The Perfect Stranger's Guide to Funerals and Grieving Practices
A Guide to Etiquette in Other People's Religious Ceremonies *Edited by Stuart M. Matlins*
6 x 9, 240 pp, Quality PB, ISBN 1-893361-20-9 **$16.95** *(A SkyLight Paths book)*

Tears of Sorrow, Seeds of Hope: A Jewish Spiritual Companion for Infertility and Pregnancy Loss *By Rabbi Nina Beth Cardin*
6 x 9, 192 pp, Hardcover, ISBN 1-58023-017-2 **$19.95**

A Time to Mourn, A Time to Comfort, 2nd Edition: A Guide to Jewish Bereavement and Comfort *By Dr. Ron Wolfson*
7 x 9, 336 pp, Quality PB, ISBN 1-58023-253-1 **$19.99**

When a Grandparent Dies: A Kid's Own Remembering Workbook for Dealing with Shiva and the Year Beyond *By Nechama Liss-Levinson, Ph.D.*
8 x 10, 48 pp, 2-color text, Hardcover, ISBN 1-879045-44-3 **$15.95** *For ages 7–13*

Abraham Joshua Heschel

The Earth Is the Lord's: The Inner World of the Jew in Eastern Europe
5½ x 8, 128 pp, Quality PB, ISBN 1-879045-42-7 **$14.95**

Israel: An Echo of Eternity New Introduction by Susannah Heschel
5½ x 8, 272 pp, Quality PB, ISBN 1-879045-70-2 **$19.95**

A Passion for Truth: Despair and Hope in Hasidism
5½ x 8, 352 pp, Quality PB, ISBN 1-879045-41-9 **$18.99**

Holidays/Holy Days

Leading the Passover Journey
The Seder's Meaning Revealed, the Haggadah's Story Retold
By Rabbi Nathan Laufer
Uncovers the hidden meaning of the Seder's rituals and customs
6 x 9, 208 pp, Hardcover, ISBN 1-58023-211-6 **$24.99**

Reclaiming Judaism as a Spiritual Practice: Holy Days and Shabbat
By Rabbi Goldie Milgram
Provides a framework for understanding the powerful and often unexplained intellectual, emotional, and spiritual tools that are essential for a lively, relevant, and fulfilling Jewish spiritual practice. 7 x 9, 272 pp, Quality PB, ISBN 1-58023-205-1 **$19.99**

7th Heaven: Celebrating Shabbat with Rebbe Nachman of Breslov
By Moshe Mykoff with the Breslov Research Institute
Explores the art of consciously observing Shabbat and understanding in-depth many of the day's spiritual practices. 5¼ x 8¼, 224 pp, Deluxe PB w/flaps, ISBN 1-58023-175-6 **$18.95**

The Women's Passover Companion
Women's Reflections on the Festival of Freedom
Edited by Rabbi Sharon Cohen Anisfeld, Tara Mohr, and Catherine Spector
Groundbreaking. A provocative conversation about women's relationships to Passover as well as the roots and meanings of women's seders.
6 x 9, 352 pp, Hardcover, ISBN 1-58023-128-4 **$24.95**

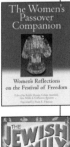

The Women's Seder Sourcebook
Rituals & Readings for Use at the Passover Seder
Edited by Rabbi Sharon Cohen Anisfeld, Tara Mohr, and Catherine Spector
Gathers the voices of more than one hundred women in readings, personal and creative reflections, commentaries, blessings, and ritual suggestions that can be incorporated into your Passover celebration.
6 x 9, 384 pp, Hardcover, ISBN 1-58023-136-5 **$24.95**

Creating Lively Passover Seders: A Sourcebook of Engaging Tales, Texts & Activities
By David Arnow, Ph.D. 7 x 9, 416 pp, Quality PB, ISBN 1-58023-184-5 **$24.99**

Hanukkah, 2nd Edition: The Family Guide to Spiritual Celebration
By Dr. Ron Wolfson. Edited by Joel Lurie Grishaver.
7 x 9, 240 pp, illus., Quality PB, ISBN 1-58023-122-5 **$18.95**

The Jewish Family Fun Book: Holiday Projects, Everyday Activities, and Travel Ideas with Jewish Themes *By Danielle Dardashti and Roni Sarig. Illus. by Avi Katz.*
6 x 9, 288 pp, 70+ b/w illus. & diagrams, Quality PB, ISBN 1-58023-171-3 **$18.95**

The Jewish Gardening Cookbook: Growing Plants & Cooking for Holidays & Festivals *By Michael Brown* 6 x 9, 224 pp, 30+ illus., Quality PB, ISBN 1-58023-116-0 **$16.95**

The Jewish Lights Book of Fun Classroom Activities: Simple and Seasonal Projects for Teachers and Students *By Danielle Dardashti and Roni Sarig*
6 x 9, 240 pp, Quality PB, ISBN 1-58023-206-X **$19.99**

Passover, 2nd Edition: The Family Guide to Spiritual Celebration
By Dr. Ron Wolfson with Joel Lurie Grishaver 7 x 9, 352 pp, Quality PB, ISBN 1-58023-174-8
$19.95

Shabbat, 2nd Edition: The Family Guide to Preparing for and Celebrating the Sabbath
By Dr. Ron Wolfson 7 x 9, 320 pp, illus., Quality PB, ISBN 1-58023-164-0 **$19.95**

Sharing Blessings: Children's Stories for Exploring the Spirit of the Jewish Holidays
By Rahel Musleah and Michael Klayman
8½ x 11, 64 pp, Full-color illus., Hardcover, ISBN 1-879045-71-0 **$18.95** *For ages 6 & up*

Inspiration

God in All Moments
Mystical & Practical Spiritual Wisdom from Hasidic Masters
Edited and translated by Or N. Rose with Ebn D. Leader
Hasidic teachings on how to be mindful in religious practice and cultivating every-day ethical behavior—*hanhagot*. 5½ x 8½, 192 pp, Quality PB, ISBN 1-58023-186-1 **$16.95**

Our Dance with God: Finding Prayer, Perspective and Meaning in the Stories of Our Lives *By Karyn D. Kedar*
Inspiring spiritual insight to guide you on your life journeys and teach you to live and thrive in two conflicting worlds: the rational/material and the spiritual.
6 x 9, 176 pp, Quality PB, ISBN 1-58023-202-7 **$16.99**

Also Available: **The Dance of the Dolphin** (Hardcover edition of *Our Dance with God*)
6 x 9, 176 pp, Hardcover, ISBN 1-58023-154-3 **$19.95**

The Empty Chair: Finding Hope and Joy—Timeless Wisdom from a Hasidic Master, Rebbe Nachman of Breslov *Adapted by Moshe Mykoff and the Breslov Research Institute*
4 x 6, 128 pp, 2-color text, Deluxe PB w/flaps, ISBN 1-879045-67-2 **$9.95**

The Gentle Weapon: Prayers for Everyday and Not-So-Everyday Moments—
Timeless Wisdom from the Teachings of the Hasidic Master, Rebbe Nachman of Breslov
Adapted by Moshe Mykoff and S. C. Mizrahi, together with the Breslov Research Institute
4 x 6, 144 pp, 2-color text, Deluxe PB w/flaps, ISBN 1-58023-022-9 **$9.95**

God Whispers: Stories of the Soul, Lessons of the Heart *By Karyn D. Kedar*
6 x 9, 176 pp, Quality PB, ISBN 1-58023-088-1 **$15.95**

An Orphan in History: One Man's Triumphant Search for His Jewish Roots
By Paul Cowan. Afterword by Rachel Cowan. 6 x 9, 288 pp, Quality PB, ISBN 1-58023-135-7 **$16.95**

Restful Reflections: Nighttime Inspiration to Calm the Soul, Based on Jewish Wisdom
By Rabbi Kerry M. Olitzky & Rabbi Lori Forman 4½ x 6¼, 448 pp, Quality PB, ISBN 1-58023-091-1 **$15.95**

Sacred Intentions: Daily Inspiration to Strengthen the Spirit, Based on Jewish Wisdom
By Rabbi Kerry M. Olitzky and Rabbi Lori Forman 4½ x 6¼, 448 pp, Quality PB, ISBN 1-58023-061-X **$15.95**

Kabbalah/Mysticism/Enneagram

Seek My Face: A Jewish Mystical Theology
By Dr. Arthur Green
This classic work of contemporary Jewish theology, revised and updated, is a profound, deeply personal statement of the lasting truths of Jewish mysticism and the basic faith claims of Judaism. A tool for anyone seeking the elusive presence of God in the world. 6 x 9, 304 pp, Quality PB, ISBN 1-58023-130-6 **$19.95**

Zohar: Annotated & Explained
Translation and annotation by Dr. Daniel C. Matt. Foreword by Andrew Harvey
Offers insightful yet unobtrusive commentary to the masterpiece of Jewish mysticism. Explains references and mystical symbols, shares wisdom of spiritual masters, and clarifies the *Zohar*'s bold claim: We have always been taught that we need God, but in order to manifest in the world, God needs us.
5½ x 8½, 160 pp, Quality PB, ISBN 1-893361-51-9 **$15.99** (A SkyLight Paths book)

Cast in God's Image: Discover Your Personality Type Using the Enneagram and Kabbalah
By Rabbi Howard A. Addison
7 x 9, 176 pp, Quality PB, Layflat binding, 20+ journaling exercises, ISBN 1-58023-124-1 **$16.95**

Ehyeh: A Kabbalah for Tomorrow *By Dr. Arthur Green*
6 x 9, 224 pp, Quality PB, ISBN 1-58023-213-2 **$16.99;** Hardcover, ISBN 1-58023-125-X **$21.95**

The Enneagram and Kabbalah: Reading Your Soul *By Rabbi Howard A. Addison*
6 x 9, 176 pp, Quality PB, ISBN 1-58023-001-6 **$15.95**

Finding Joy: A Practical Spiritual Guide to Happiness *By Dannel I. Schwartz with Mark Hass*
6 x 9, 192 pp, Quality PB, ISBN 1-58023-009-1 **$14.95**

The Gift of Kabbalah: Discovering the Secrets of Heaven, Renewing Your Life on Earth
By Tamar Frankiel, Ph.D.
6 x 9, 256 pp, Quality PB, ISBN 1-58023-141-1 **$16.95;** Hardcover, ISBN 1-58023-108-X **$21.95**

The Way Into Jewish Mystical Tradition *By Lawrence Kushner*
6 x 9, 224 pp, Quality PB, ISBN 1-58023-200-0 **$18.99;** Hardcover, ISBN 1-58023-029-6 **$21.95**

Life Cycle
Marriage / Parenting / Family / Aging

Jewish Fathers: A Legacy of Love
Photographs by Lloyd Wolf. Essays by Paula Wolfson. Foreword by Harold S. Kushner.
Honors the role of contemporary Jewish fathers in America. Each father tells in his own words what it means to be a parent and Jewish, and what he learned from his own father. Insightful photos. 9½ x 9⅞, 144 pp with 100+ duotone photos, Hardcover, ISBN 1-58023-204-3 **$30.00**

The New Jewish Baby Album: Creating and Celebrating the Beginning of a Spiritual Life—A Jewish Lights Companion
By the Editors at Jewish Lights. Foreword by Anita Diamant. Preface by Sandy Eisenberg Sasso.
A spiritual keepsake that will be treasured for generations. More than just a memory book, *shows you how—and why it's important*—to create a Jewish home and a Jewish life. 8 x 10, 64 pp, Deluxe Padded Hardcover, Full-color illus., ISBN 1-58023-138-1 **$19.95**

The Jewish Pregnancy Book: A Resource for the Soul, Body & Mind during Pregnancy, Birth & the First Three Months
By Sandy Falk, M.D., and Rabbi Daniel Judson, with Steven A. Rapp
Includes medical information, prayers and rituals for each stage of pregnancy, from a liberal Jewish perspective. 7 x 10, 208 pp, Quality PB, b/w illus., ISBN 1-58023-178-0 **$16.95**

Celebrating Your New Jewish Daughter: Creating Jewish Ways to Welcome Baby Girls into the Covenant—New and Traditional Ceremonies
By Debra Nussbaum Cohen 6 x 9, 272 pp, Quality PB, ISBN 1-58023-090-3 **$18.95**

The New Jewish Baby Book, 2nd Edition: Names, Ceremonies & Customs—A Guide for Today's Families *By Anita Diamant* 6 x 9, 336 pp, Quality PB, ISBN 1-58023-251-5 **$19.99**

Parenting As a Spiritual Journey: Deepening Ordinary and Extraordinary Events into Sacred Occasions *By Rabbi Nancy Fuchs-Kreimer* 6 x 9, 224 pp, Quality PB, ISBN 1-58023-016-4 **$16.95**

Judaism for Two: A Spiritual Guide for Strengthening and Celebrating Your Loving Relationship *By Rabbi Nancy Fuchs-Kreimer and Rabbi Nancy H. Wiener*
Addresses the ways Jewish teachings can enhance and strengthen committed relationships. 6 x 9, 208 pp, Quality PB, ISBN 1-58023-254-X **$16.99**

Embracing the Covenant: Converts to Judaism Talk About Why & How
By Rabbi Allan Berkowitz and Patti Moskovitz 6 x 9, 192 pp, Quality PB, ISBN 1-879045-50-8 **$16.95**

The Guide to Jewish Interfaith Family Life: An InterfaithFamily.com Handbook
Edited by Ronnie Friedland and Edmund Case 6 x 9, 384 pp, Quality PB, ISBN 1-58023-153-5
$18.95

Introducing My Faith and My Community
The Jewish Outreach Institute Guide for the Christian in a Jewish Interfaith Relationship
By Rabbi Kerry M. Olitzky 6 x 9, 176 pp, Quality PB, ISBN 1-58023-192-6 **$16.99**

Making a Successful Jewish Interfaith Marriage: The Jewish Outreach Institute Guide to Opportunities, Challenges and Resources
By Rabbi Kerry M. Olitzky with Joan Peterson Littman 6 x 9, 176 pp, Quality PB, ISBN 1-58023-170-5 **$16.95**

The Creative Jewish Wedding Book: A Hands-On Guide to New & Old Traditions, Ceremonies & Celebrations *By Gabrielle Kaplan-Mayer*
Provides the tools to create the most meaningful Jewish traditional or alternative wedding by using ritual elements to express your unique style and spirituality. 9 x 9, 288 pp, b/w photos, Quality PB, ISBN 1-58023-194-2 **$19.99**

Divorce Is a Mitzvah: A Practical Guide to Finding Wholeness and Holiness When Your Marriage Dies *By Rabbi Perry Netter. Afterword by Rabbi Laura Geller.*
6 x 9, 224 pp, Quality PB, ISBN 1-58023-172-1 **$16.95**

A Heart of Wisdom: Making the Jewish Journey from Midlife through the Elder Years
Edited by Susan Berrin. Foreword by Harold Kushner. 6 x 9, 384 pp, Quality PB, ISBN 1-58023-051-2 **$18.95**

So That Your Values Live On: Ethical Wills and How to Prepare Them
Edited by Jack Riemer and Nathaniel Stampfer 6 x 9, 272 pp, Quality PB, ISBN 1-879045-34-6 **$18.95**

Meditation

The Handbook of Jewish Meditation Practices
A Guide for Enriching the Sabbath and Other Days of Your Life
By Rabbi David A. Cooper
Easy-to-learn meditation techniques. 6 x 9, 208 pp, Quality PB, ISBN 1-58023-102-0 **$16.95**

Discovering Jewish Meditation: Instruction & Guidance for Learning an Ancient
Spiritual Practice *By Nan Fink Gefen, Ph.D.* 6 x 9, 208 pp, Quality PB, ISBN 1-58023-067-9
$16.95

A Heart of Stillness: A Complete Guide to Learning the Art of Meditation
By Rabbi David A. Cooper 5½ x 8½, 272 pp, Quality PB, ISBN 1-893361-03-9 **$16.95**
(A SkyLight Paths book)

Meditation from the Heart of Judaism: Today's Teachers Share Their
Practices, Techniques, and Faith *Edited by Avram Davis*
6 x 9, 256 pp, Quality PB, ISBN 1-58023-049-0 **$16.95**

Silence, Simplicity & Solitude: A Complete Guide to Spiritual Retreat at Home
By Rabbi David A. Cooper 5½ x 8½, 336 pp, Quality PB, ISBN 1-893361-04-7 **$16.95**
(A SkyLight Paths book)

The Way of Flame: A Guide to the Forgotten Mystical Tradition of Jewish
Meditation *By Avram Davis* 4½ x 8, 176 pp, Quality PB, ISBN 1-58023-060-1 **$15.95**

Ritual/Sacred Practice/Journaling

The Jewish Dream Book: The Key to Opening the Inner Meaning of
Your Dreams *By Vanessa L. Ochs with Elizabeth Ochs; Full-color illus. by Kristina Swarner*
Instructions for how modern people can perform ancient Jewish dream practices
and dream interpretations drawn from the Jewish wisdom tradition. For anyone
who wants to understand their dreams—and themselves.
8 x 8, 120 pp, Full-color illus., Deluxe PB w/flaps, ISBN 1-58023-132-2 **$16.95**

The Jewish Journaling Book: How to Use Jewish Tradition to Write
Your Life & Explore Your Soul *By Janet Ruth Falon*
Details the history of Jewish journaling throughout biblical and modern times,
and teaches specific journaling techniques to help you create and maintain a vital
journal, from a Jewish perspective. 8 x 8, 304 pp, Deluxe PB w/flaps, ISBN 1-58023-203-5 **$18.99**

The Book of Jewish Sacred Practices: CLAL's Guide to Everyday & Holiday
Rituals & Blessings *Edited by Rabbi Irwin Kula and Vanessa L. Ochs, Ph.D.*
6 x 9, 368 pp, Quality PB, ISBN 1-58023-152-7 **$18.95**

Jewish Ritual: A Brief Introduction for Christians
By Rabbi Kerry M. Olitzky and Rabbi Daniel Judson
5½ x 8½, 144 pp, Quality PB, ISBN 1-58023-210-8 **$14.99**

The Rituals & Practices of a Jewish Life: A Handbook for Personal Spiritual
Renewal *Edited by Rabbi Kerry M. Olitzky and Rabbi Daniel Judson*
6 x 9, 272 pp, illus., Quality PB, ISBN 1-58023-169-1 **$18.95**

Science Fiction/
Mystery & Detective Fiction

Mystery Midrash: An Anthology of Jewish Mystery & Detective Fiction
Edited by Lawrence W. Raphael. Preface by Joel Siegel.
6 x 9, 304 pp, Quality PB, ISBN 1-58023-055-5 **$16.95**

Criminal Kabbalah: An Intriguing Anthology of Jewish Mystery & Detective Fiction
Edited by Lawrence W. Raphael. Foreword by Laurie R. King.
6 x 9, 256 pp, Quality PB, ISBN 1-58023-109-8 **$16.95**

More Wandering Stars: An Anthology of Outstanding Stories of Jewish Fantasy and
Science Fiction *Edited by Jack Dann. Introduction by Isaac Asimov.*
6 x 9, 192 pp, Quality PB, ISBN 1-58023-063-6 **$16.95**

Wandering Stars: An Anthology of Jewish Fantasy & Science Fiction
Edited by Jack Dann. Introduction by Isaac Asimov.
6 x 9, 272 pp, Quality PB, ISBN 1-58023-005-9 **$16.95**

Spirituality

Does the Soul Survive?: A Jewish Journey to Belief in Afterlife, Past
Lives & Living with Purpose *By Rabbi Elie Kaplan Spitz. Foreword by Brian L Weiss, M.D.*
Spitz relates his own experiences and those shared with him by people he has
worked with as a rabbi, and shows us that belief in afterlife and past lives, so
often approached with reluctance, is in fact true to Jewish tradition.
6 x 9, 288 pp, Quality PB, ISBN 1-58023-165-9 **$16.95**; Hardcover, ISBN 1-58023-094-6 **$21.95**

First Steps to a New Jewish Spirit: Reb Zalman's Guide to
Recapturing the Intimacy & Ecstasy in Your Relationship with God
By Rabbi Zalman M. Schachter-Shalomi with Donald Gropman
An extraordinary spiritual handbook that restores psychic and physical vigor by
introducing us to new models and alternative ways of practicing Judaism. Offers
meditation and contemplation exercises for enriching the most important aspects
of everyday life. 6 x 9, 144 pp, Quality PB, ISBN 1-58023-182-9 **$16.95**

God in Our Relationships: Spirituality between People from the
Teachings of Martin Buber *By Rabbi Dennis S. Ross*
On the eightieth anniversary of Buber's classic work, we can discover new
answers to critical issues in our lives. Inspiring examples from Ross's own life—
as congregational rabbi, father, hospital chaplain, social worker, and husband—
illustrate Buber's difficult-to-understand ideas about how we encounter God and
each other. 5½ x 8½, 160 pp, Quality PB, ISBN 1-58023-147-0 **$16.95**

Judaism, Physics and God: Searching for Sacred Metaphors in
a Post-Einstein World *By Rabbi David W. Nelson*
In clear, non-technical terms, this provocative fusion of religion and science
examines the great theories of modern physics to find new ways for contemporary people to express their spiritual beliefs and thoughts.
6 x 9, 352 pp, Hardcover, ISBN 1-58023-252-3 **$24.99**

The Jewish Lights Spirituality Handbook: A Guide to Understanding,
Exploring & Living a Spiritual Life *Edited by Stuart M. Matlins*
What exactly is "Jewish" about spirituality? How do I make it a part of my life?
Fifty of today's foremost spiritual leaders share their ideas and experience with us.
6 x 9, 456 pp, Quality PB, ISBN 1-58023-093-8 **$19.95**; Hardcover, ISBN 1-58023-100-4 **$24.95**

Bringing the Psalms to Life: How to Understand and Use the Book of Psalms
By Dr. Daniel F. Polish
6 x 9, 208 pp, Quality PB, ISBN 1-58023-157-8 **$16.95**; Hardcover, ISBN 1-58023-077-6 **$21.95**

God & the Big Bang: Discovering Harmony between Science & Spirituality
By Dr. Daniel C. Matt 6 x 9, 216 pp, Quality PB, ISBN 1-879045-89-3 **$16.95**

Godwrestling—Round 2: Ancient Wisdom, Future Paths
By Rabbi Arthur Waskow 6 x 9, 352 pp, Quality PB, ISBN 1-879045-72-9 **$18.95**

One God Clapping: The Spiritual Path of a Zen Rabbi *By Rabbi Alan Lew with Sherril Jaffe*
5½ x 8½, 336 pp, Quality PB, ISBN 1-58023-115-2 **$16.95**

The Path of Blessing: Experiencing the Energy and Abundance of the Divine
By Rabbi Marcia Prager 5½ x 8½, 240 pp., Quality PB, ISBN 1-58023-148-9 **$16.95**

Six Jewish Spiritual Paths: A Rationalist Looks at Spirituality *By Rabbi Rifat Sonsino*
6 x 9, 208 pp, Quality PB, ISBN 1-58023-167-5 **$16.95**; Hardcover, ISBN 1-58023-095-4 **$21.95**

Soul Judaism: Dancing with God into a New Era
By Rabbi Wayne Dosick 5½ x 8½, 304 pp, Quality PB, ISBN 1-58023-053-9 **$16.95**

Stepping Stones to Jewish Spiritual Living: Walking the Path Morning, Noon,
and Night *By Rabbi James L. Mirel and Karen Bonnell Werth*
6 x 9, 240 pp, Quality PB, ISBN 1-58023-074-1 **$16.95**; Hardcover, ISBN 1-58023-003-2 **$21.95**

There Is No Messiah... and You're It: The Stunning Transformation of Judaism's
Most Provocative Idea *By Rabbi Robert N. Levine, D.D.*
6 x 9, 192 pp, Quality PB, ISBN 1-58023-255-8 **$16.99**; Hardcover, ISBN 1-58023-173-X **$21.95**

These Are the Words: A Vocabulary of Jewish Spiritual Life *By Dr. Arthur Green*
6 x 9, 304 pp, Quality PB, ISBN 1-58023-107-1 **$18.95**

Spirituality/Lawrence Kushner

Filling Words with Light: Hasidic and Mystical Reflections on Jewish Prayer
By Lawrence Kushner and Nehemia Polen
Reflects on the joy, gratitude, mystery, and awe embedded in traditional prayers and blessings, and shows how you can imbue these familiar sacred words with your own sense of holiness. 5½ x 8½, 176 pp, Hardcover, ISBN 1-58023-216-7 **$21.99**

The Book of Letters: A Mystical Hebrew Alphabet
Popular Hardcover Edition, 6 x 9, 80 pp, 2-color text, ISBN 1-879045-00-1 **$24.95**
Collector's Limited Edition, 9 x 12, 80 pp, gold foil embossed pages, w/limited edition silkscreened print, ISBN 1-879045-04-4 **$349.00**

The Book of Miracles: A Young Person's Guide to Jewish Spiritual Awareness
  6 x 9, 96 pp, 2-color illus., Hardcover, ISBN 1-879045-78-8 **$16.95** *For ages 9–13*

The Book of Words: Talking Spiritual Life, Living Spiritual Talk
  6 x 9, 160 pp, Quality PB, ISBN 1-58023-020-2 **$16.95**

Eyes Remade for Wonder: A Lawrence Kushner Reader *Introduction by Thomas Moore*
  6 x 9, 240 pp, Quality PB, ISBN 1-58023-042-3 **$18.95;** Hardcover, ISBN 1-58023-014-8 **$23.95**

God Was in This Place & I, i Did Not Know
Finding Self, Spirituality and Ultimate Meaning 6 x 9, 192 pp, Quality PB, ISBN 1-879045-33-8 **$16.95**

Honey from the Rock: An Introduction to Jewish Mysticism
  6 x 9, 176 pp, Quality PB, ISBN 1-58023-073-3 **$16.95**

Invisible Lines of Connection: Sacred Stories of the Ordinary
  5½ x 8½, 160 pp, Quality PB, ISBN 1-879045-98-2 **$15.95**

Jewish Spirituality—A Brief Introduction for Christians
  5½ x 8½, 112 pp, Quality PB Original, ISBN 1-58023-150-0 **$12.95**

The River of Light: Jewish Mystical Awareness 6 x 9, 192 pp, Quality PB, ISBN 1-58023-096-2 **$16.95**

The Way Into Jewish Mystical Tradition
  6 x 9, 224 pp, Quality PB, ISBN 1-58023-200-0 **$18.99;** Hardcover, ISBN 1-58023-029-6 **$21.95**

Spirituality/Prayer

Pray Tell: A Hadassah Guide to Jewish Prayer
By Rabbi Jules Harlow, with contributions from Tamara Cohen, Rochelle Furstenberg, Rabbi Daniel Gordis, Leora Tanenbaum, and many others
A guide to traditional Jewish prayer enriched with insight and wisdom from a broad variety of viewpoints—from Orthodox, Conservative, Reform, and Reconstructionist Judaism to New Age and feminist.
8½ x 11, 400 pp, Quality PB, ISBN 1-58023-163-2 **$29.95**

My People's Prayer Book Series

Traditional Prayers, Modern Commentaries *Edited by Rabbi Lawrence A. Hoffman*
Provides diverse and exciting commentary to the traditional liturgy, helping modern men and women find new wisdom in Jewish prayer, and bring liturgy into their lives.

Each book includes Hebrew text, modern translation, and commentaries from all perspectives of the Jewish world.
Vol. 1—The *Sh'ma* and Its Blessings
7 x 10, 168 pp, Hardcover, ISBN 1-879045-79-6 **$24.99**
Vol. 2—The *Amidah*
7 x 10, 240 pp, Hardcover, ISBN 1-879045-80-X **$24.95**
Vol. 3—*P'sukei D'zimrah* (Morning Psalms)
7 x 10, 240 pp, Hardcover, ISBN 1-879045-81-8 **$24.95**
Vol. 4—*Seder K'riat Hatorah* (The Torah Service)
7 x 10, 264 pp, Hardcover, ISBN 1-879045-82-6 **$23.95**
Vol. 5—*Birkhot Hashachar* (Morning Blessings)
7 x 10, 240 pp, Hardcover, ISBN 1-879045-83-4 **$24.95**
Vol. 6—*Tachanun* and Concluding Prayers
7 x 10, 240 pp, Hardcover, ISBN 1-879045-84-2 **$24.95**
Vol. 7—Shabbat at Home
7 x 10, 240 pp, Hardcover, ISBN 1-879045-85-0 **$24.95**
Vol. 8—*Kabbalat Shabbat* (Welcoming Shabbat in the Synagogue)
7 x 10, 240 pp, Hardcover, ISBN 1-58023-121-7 **$24.99**

Spirituality/Women's Interest

The Quotable Jewish Woman: Wisdom, Inspiration & Humor from the Mind & Heart *Edited and compiled by Elaine Bernstein Partnow*
The definitive collection of ideas, reflections, humor, and wit of over 300 Jewish women.
6 x 9, 496 pp, Hardcover, ISBN 1-58023-193-4 **$29.99**

Lifecycles, Vol. 1: Jewish Women on Life Passages & Personal Milestones
Edited and with introductions by Rabbi Debra Orenstein 6 x 9, 480 pp, Quality PB, ISBN 1-58023-018-0 **$19.95**
Lifecycles, Vol. 2: Jewish Women on Biblical Themes in Contemporary Life
Edited and with introductions by Rabbi Debra Orenstein and Rabbi Jane Rachel Litman
6 x 9, 464 pp, Quality PB, ISBN 1-58023-019-9 **$19.95**
Moonbeams: A Hadassah Rosh Hodesh Guide *Edited by Carol Diament, Ph.D.*
8½ x 11, 240 pp, Quality PB, ISBN 1-58023-099-7 **$20.00**
ReVisions: Seeing Torah through a Feminist Lens *By Rabbi Elyse Goldstein*
5½ x 8½, 224 pp, Quality PB, ISBN 1-58023-117-9 **$16.95**

White Fire: A Portrait of Women Spiritual Leaders in America
By Rabbi Malka Drucker. Photographs by Gay Block.
7 x 10, 320 pp, 30+ b/w photos, Hardcover, ISBN 1-893361-64-0 **$24.95** *(A SkyLight Paths book)*
Women of the Wall: Claiming Sacred Ground at Judaism's Holy Site
Edited by Phyllis Chesler and Rivka Haut 6 x 9, 496 pp, b/w photos, Hardcover, ISBN 1-58023-161-6 **$34.95**

The Women's Haftarah Commentary: New Insights from Women Rabbis on the 54 Weekly Haftarah Portions, the 5 Megillot & Special Shabbatot
Edited by Rabbi Elyse Goldstein 6 x 9, 560 pp, Hardcover, ISBN 1-58023-133-0 **$39.99**
The Women's Torah Commentary: New Insights from Women Rabbis on the 54 Weekly Torah Portions *Edited by Rabbi Elyse Goldstein*
6 x 9, 496 pp, Hardcover, ISBN 1-58023-076-8 **$34.95**
The Year Mom Got Religion: One Woman's Midlife Journey into Judaism
By Lee Meyerhoff Hendler 6 x 9, 208 pp, Quality PB, ISBN 1-58023-070-9 **$15.95**

See Holidays for *The Women's Passover Companion: Women's Reflections on the Festival of Freedom* and *The Women's Seder Sourcebook: Rituals & Readings for Use at the Passover Seder.* Also see Bar/Bat Mitzvah for *The JGirl's Guide: The Young Jewish Woman's Handbook for Coming of Age.*

Travel

Israel—A Spiritual Travel Guide, 2nd Edition
A Companion for the Modern Jewish Pilgrim
By Rabbi Lawrence A. Hoffman 4¾ x 10, 256 pp, Quality PB, illus., ISBN 1-58023-261-2 **$18.99**
Also Available: **The Israel Mission Leader's Guide** ISBN 1-58023-085-7 **$4.95**

12 Steps

100 Blessings Every Day Daily Twelve Step Recovery Affirmations, Exercises for Personal Growth & Renewal Reflecting Seasons of the Jewish Year
By Rabbi Kerry M. Olitzky. Foreword by Rabbi Neil Gillman.
One-day-at-a-time monthly format. Reflects on the rhythm of the Jewish calendar to bring insight to recovery from addictions.
4½ x 6¼, 432 pp, Quality PB, ISBN 1-879045-30-3 **$15.99**

Recovery from Codependence: A Jewish Twelve Steps Guide to Healing Your Soul
By Rabbi Kerry M. Olitzky 6 x 9, 160 pp, Quality PB, ISBN 1-879045-32-X **$13.95**
Renewed Each Day: Daily Twelve Step Recovery Meditations Based on the Bible
By Rabbi Kerry M. Olitzky and Aaron Z.
Vol. 1—Genesis & Exodus: 6 x 9, 224 pp, Quality PB, ISBN 1-879045-12-5 **$14.95**
Vol. 2—Leviticus, Numbers & Deuteronomy: 6 x 9, 280 pp, Quality PB, ISBN 1-879045-13-3 **$14.95**
Twelve Jewish Steps to Recovery: A Personal Guide to Turning from Alcoholism & Other Addictions—Drugs, Food, Gambling, Sex...
By Rabbi Kerry M. Olitzky and Stuart A. Copans, M.D. Preface by Abraham J. Twerski, M.D.
6 x 9, 144 pp, Quality PB, ISBN 1-879045-09-5 **$14.95**

Spirituality/The Way Into... Series

The Way Into... Series offers an accessible and highly usable "guided tour" of the Jewish faith, people, history and beliefs—in total, an introduction to Judaism that will enable you to understand and interact with the sacred texts of the Jewish tradition. Each volume is written by a leading contemporary scholar and teacher, and explores one key aspect of Judaism. The Way Into... enables all readers to achieve a real sense of Jewish cultural literacy through guided study.

The Way Into Encountering God in Judaism By Neil Gillman
6 x 9, 240 pp, Quality PB, ISBN 1-58023-199-3 **$18.99**; Hardcover, ISBN 1-58023-025-3 **$21.95**

Also Available: **The Jewish Approach to God: A Brief Introduction for Christians**
By Neil Gillman 5½ x 8½, 192 pp, Quality PB, ISBN 1-58023-190-X **$16.95**

The Way Into Jewish Mystical Tradition By Lawrence Kushner
6 x 9, 224 pp, Quality PB, ISBN 1-58023-200-0 **$18.99**; Hardcover, ISBN 1-58023-029-6 **$21.95**

The Way Into Jewish Prayer By Lawrence A. Hoffman
6 x 9, 224 pp, Quality PB, ISBN 1-58023-201-9 **$18.99**; Hardcover, ISBN 1-58023-027-X **$21.95**

The Way Into Torah By Norman J. Cohen
6 x 9, 176 pp, Quality PB, ISBN 1-58023-198-5 **$16.99**; Hardcover, ISBN 1-58023-028-8 **$21.95**

Spirituality in the Workplace

Being God's Partner
How to Find the Hidden Link Between Spirituality and Your Work
By Rabbi Jeffrey K. Salkin. Introduction by Norman Lear.
6 x 9, 192 pp, Quality PB, ISBN 1-879045-65-6 **$17.95**

The Business Bible: 10 New Commandments for Bringing Spirituality & Ethical Values into the Workplace By Rabbi Wayne Dosick
5½ x 8½, 208 pp, Quality PB, ISBN 1-58023-101-2 **$14.95**

Spirituality and Wellness

Aleph-Bet Yoga
Embodying the Hebrew Letters for Physical and Spiritual Well-Being
By Steven A. Rapp. Foreword by Tamar Frankiel, Ph.D., and Judy Greenfeld. Preface by Hart Lazer
7 x 10, 128 pp, b/w photos, Quality PB, Layflat binding, ISBN 1-58023-162-6 **$16.95**

Entering the Temple of Dreams
Jewish Prayers, Movements, and Meditations for the End of the Day
By Tamar Frankiel, Ph.D., and Judy Greenfeld
7 x 10, 192 pp, illus., Quality PB, ISBN 1-58023-079-2 **$16.95**

Jewish Paths toward Healing and Wholeness: A Personal Guide to Dealing with Suffering By Rabbi Kerry M. Olitzky. Foreword by Debbie Friedman.
6 x 9, 192 pp, Quality PB, ISBN 1-58023-068-7 **$15.95**

Minding the Temple of the Soul
Balancing Body, Mind, and Spirit through Traditional Jewish Prayer, Movement, and Meditation By Tamar Frankiel, Ph.D., and Judy Greenfeld
7 x 10, 184 pp, illus., Quality PB, ISBN 1-879045-64-8 **$16.95**
Audiotape of the Blessings and Meditations: 60 min. **$9.95**
Videotape of the Movements and Meditations: 46 min. **$20.00**

Theology/Philosophy

Aspects of Rabbinic Theology
By Solomon Schechter. New Introduction by Dr. Neil Gillman.
6 x 9, 448 pp, Quality PB, ISBN 1-879045-24-9 **$19.95**

Broken Tablets: Restoring the Ten Commandments and Ourselves
Edited by Rachel S. Mikva. Introduction by Lawrence Kushner. Afterword by Arnold Jacob Wolf.
6 x 9, 192 pp, Quality PB, ISBN 1-58023-158-6 **$16.95**; Hardcover, ISBN 1-58023-066-0 **$21.95**

Creating an Ethical Jewish Life
A Practical Introduction to Classic Teachings on How to Be a Jew
By Dr. Byron L. Sherwin and Seymour J. Cohen
6 x 9, 336 pp, Quality PB, ISBN 1-58023-114-4 **$19.95**

The Death of Death: Resurrection and Immortality in Jewish Thought
By Dr. Neil Gillman 6 x 9, 336 pp, Quality PB, ISBN 1-58023-081-4 **$18.95**

Evolving Halakhah: A Progressive Approach to Traditional Jewish Law
By Rabbi Dr. Moshe Zemer
6 x 9, 480 pp, Quality PB, ISBN 1-58023-127-6 **$29.95**; Hardcover, ISBN 1-58023-002-4 **$40.00**

Hasidic Tales: Annotated & Explained
By Rabbi Rami Shapiro. Foreword by Andrew Harvey, SkyLight Illuminations series editor.
5¼ x 8¼, 240 pp, Quality PB, ISBN 1-893361-86-1 **$16.95** *(A SkyLight Paths Book)*

A Heart of Many Rooms: Celebrating the Many Voices within Judaism
By Dr. David Hartman 6 x 9, 352 pp, Quality PB, ISBN 1-58023-156-X **$19.95**

The Hebrew Prophets: Selections Annotated & Explained
Translation & Annotation by Rabbi Rami Shapiro. Foreword by Zalman M. Schachter-Shalomi
5½ x 8½, 224 pp, Quality PB, ISBN 1-59473-037-7 **$16.99** *(A SkyLight Paths book)*

Keeping Faith with the Psalms: Deepen Your Relationship with God Using the
Book of Psalms *By Daniel F. Polish* 6 x 9, 272 pp, Hardcover, ISBN 1-58023-179-9 **$24.95**

The Last Trial
On the Legends and Lore of the Command to Abraham to Offer Isaac as a Sacrifice
By Shalom Spiegel. New Introduction by Judah Goldin.
6 x 9, 208 pp, Quality PB, ISBN 1-879045-29-X **$18.95**

A Living Covenant: The Innovative Spirit in Traditional Judaism
By Dr. David Hartman 6 x 9, 368 pp, Quality PB, ISBN 1-58023-011-3 **$18.95**

Love and Terror in the God Encounter
The Theological Legacy of Rabbi Joseph B. Soloveitchik
By Dr. David Hartman
6 x 9, 240 pp, Quality PB, ISBN 1-58023-176-4 **$19.95**; Hardcover, ISBN 1-58023-112-8 **$25.00**

Seeking the Path to Life
Theological Meditations on God and the Nature of People, Love, Life and Death
By Rabbi Ira F. Stone 6 x 9, 160 pp, Quality PB, ISBN 1-879045-47-8 **$14.95**

The Spirit of Renewal: Finding Faith after the Holocaust
By Rabbi Edward Feld 6 x 9, 224 pp, Quality PB, ISBN 1-879045-40-0 **$16.95**

Tormented Master: *The Life and Spiritual Quest of Rabbi Nahman of Bratslav*
By Dr. Arthur Green 6 x 9, 416 pp, Quality PB, ISBN 1-879045-11-7 **$19.99**

Your Word Is Fire: The Hasidic Masters on Contemplative Prayer
Edited and translated by Dr. Arthur Green and Barry W. Holtz
6 x 9, 160 pp, Quality PB, ISBN 1-879045-25-7 **$15.95**

I Am Jewish
Personal Reflections Inspired by the Last Words of Daniel Pearl
Almost 150 Jews—both famous and not—from all walks of life, from all around
the world, write about Identity, Heritage, Covenant / Chosenness and Faith,
Humanity and Ethnicity, and *Tikkun Olam* and Justice.
Edited by Judea and Ruth Pearl
6 x 9, 304 pp, Deluxe PB w/flaps, ISBN 1-58023-259-0 **$18.99**; Hardcover, ISBN 1-58023-183-7 **$24.99**
Download a free copy of the *I Am Jewish Teacher's Guide* at our website:
www.jewishlights.com